Written by **Doug Small**
Cover Design: **Sarah Nesenjuk**
Book Design & Photo Research: **Sarah Nesenjuk**

Front Cover: **Jenny Lewis** / Retna Ltd / Camera Press
Back Cover: **Frank White**
Photo Credits: **Cortes Jody Anthony** / Corbis: 26 & 41 • **Siemoneit Ashford** / Corbis: 54 •
Jay Blakesberg / Retna : 11, 12, 22, 23 & 41 • **Cameron Bloom** / LFI: 42 • **Awais Butt** / LFI: 78 •
Corbis / Corbis: 32 • **David Fisher** / LFI: 56, 80 & 84 • **Mitchell Gerber** / Corbis: 57 •
Tony J. Haresign / LFI: 75 • **Paul Harness** / LFI: 55b • **Rune Hellestad** / Corbis: 1 •
London Features / LFI: 52 & 55t • **Jen Lowery** / LFI: 14, 54, 86, & 98 • **Bruno Marzi** / LFI: 60 •
Sean Murphy / Camera Press: 74 • **NGMH** / LFI: 4 & 5 • **Martin Philbey** / Corbis: 72, 94 & 100 •
Neal Preston / Retna: 31 • **Derek Ridgers** / LFI: 46 & 49 • **S.I.N.** / Corbis: 3 • **Kelly A. Swift** / Retna: 91 •
Frank Trapper / Corbis: 53 • **Frank White**: 8, 18, 20, 34, 36, 38, 43, 44, 50, 51, 53, 62, 64, 65, 69, 76, 88
& 102 • **Michael Williams** / LFI: 85 & 92 • **Katy Winn** / Corbis: 50

Omnibus Press
A Division of Music Sales Corporation, New York

Exclusive Distributors:
Music Sales Corporation
257 Park Avenue South, New York, NY 10010 USA
Music Sales Limited
8/9 Frith Street, London W1D 3JB England
Music Sales Pty. Limited
120 Rothschild Street, Rosebery, Sydney, NSW 2018, Australia

Order No. OP 51084
International Standard Book Number: 0.8256.3408.3

Printed in the United States of America

Omnibus Press Presents the Story of

GREEN DAY

by Doug Small

OMNIBUS PRESS
LONDON · NEW YORK · SYDNEY

Contents

INTRODUCTION p.6 / SWEET CHILDREN p.9 / LOOK OUT! p.15 / KERPLUNKED p.21 / PARADISE BLAST p.25 / LONGV

A WARPED WARNING p.63 / KNOWLEDGE p.71 / RARITIES p.77 / OF RAGE AND LOVE p.81 / AMERICAN IDIOT p.89

29 / OUT SOLD p.35 / WALKING EQUILIBRIUM p.39 / HITCHIN' A RIOT p.45 / WAKE UP p.59 /
EART-SHAPED HAND GRENADE p.95 / GODFATHERS p.101 / U.S. DISCOGRAPHY p.103

Long ago and far away, in a grunge-obsessed land known as America circa 1994, punk rock vaguely brought to mind the Ramones and the Sex Pistols. . .and then the *Dookie* hit the fan. California punk trio Green Day took the music scene by complete surprise with their major-label debut album that jumpstarted a new punk revolution and went on to sell well over ten million copies. The bratty band and its baby-faced, blue-haired lead singer with a sneer found themselves spitting and pogoing their

way to the top of the charts, dragging an entire subculture into the spotlight along with them. The pairing of catchy melodies with unrelenting power-chords and a Johnny Rottenesque accent and attitude earned Green Day the label "pop-punk," and unwittingly fostered a veritable crop of bands in the newly created genre.

Frontman and guitarist Billie Joe Armstrong, bassist Mike Dirnt, and drummer Tré Cool had

actually been writing songs, playing live, and living in punk squats since most kids their age were still trying to get out of doing their homework. The Berkeley band may have been new to the world of high-rotation MTV coverage and sold out stadiums, but they had been touring and releasing records since they were teenagers. That guitar covered in stickers, dirt, and the initials B.J. in the breakthrough "Longview" video looked beat up for a reason.

Fast forward one decade. Green Day had in the interim released three more studio albums, a greatest hits collection, a rarities compilation, and were known to deliver exceptional singles with equally riveting music videos. Through relentless touring around the globe, their ever-burgeoning fan base barely had time to cheer (or trade expletives with Billie Joe) between each manic three-minute treatment of tunes so irresistible they threatened to wipe the scowl off even the most self-respecting punk rocker's face. Barely in their thirties, the three elder statesmen could have sat back on their punk laurels and no one would have blamed them.

Instead they decided to knock the music industry sideways once again, and delivered 2004's *American Idiot*, a self-declared punk-rock opera that took on the government. The record debuted at no less than Number One around the world and garnered universal critical acclaim the likes of which most bands dare not dream.

SWEET CHILDREN

Rodeo, California, a mere fifteen miles north of happening hotspot Berkeley—cosmopolitan, liberal-leaning home of the University of California—may just as well have been fifteen thousand miles away. The isolated outpost had little to offer for any punk-minded youth with an ounce of creativity. The community, comprised mainly of massive chemical and oil refineries and modest houses, appears harmless enough, but despite the proliferation of churches and American flags, beneath the whole-some-enough image was an active drug culture. As in many of America's rural and suburban communities, boredom-bred substance abuse was a common recourse amongst the town's youth. Billie Joe declared his hometown "the most unscenic place on the planet" in a December 23, 1994 *Entertainment Weekly* article, and went on to add, "We went to this elementary school, and they used to always send kids home with headaches. They figured it was because of the toxins that the refineries were throwing in the air." Memories. . .

From the ripe old age of five, Billie Joe—born February 17, 1972—exhibited a musical bent and his first "tour" consisted of gigs singing in children's hospitals and old people's homes. He even released a single: A song called "Look for Love" penned by James and Marie Louise Fiatarone and released on Fiat Records in 1977. The black vinyl seven-inch features an interview with the young crooner entitled "Meet Billie Joe." When the young punk-to-be was just nine years old, he saw the Ramones' film *Rock 'n' Roll High School*. Years later in an April 17, 2001 MTV interview he was to remember the lasting impression this early glimpse into the music scene had on him, saying, "To me, what I saw was the perfect rock band. They had songs that just stuck in your head. Just like a hammer, they banged right into your brain."

"Music has always been in my household, whether it was my dad playing jazz, or my sister playing clarinet or something like that," Billie Joe told *Guitar World* in its February/March 2005 issue. "And we always had an acoustic guitar around the house—just a piece-of-sh*t nylon-string. . .just laying around for me to toy with." His father, who earned a living as a truck driver, managed to sandwich in stints as a jazz drummer. His mother was a diehard country-music fan. Billie Joe was the youngest of the six Armstrong kids. "Mom gradually got less strict with each kid," he confessed to *Time* magazine in a June 27, 1994 article. When he was just ten years old, his father died of cancer in September of 1982. The big happy family was suddenly thrown into chaos, as Billie Joe's mother was forced to waitress full-time and subsequently remarried, introducing a rather unwelcome stepfather into the mix.

It was during this tumultuous time that Billie Joe formed a strong friendship with a grade-school classmate named Mike Pritchard (to become Dirnt). The two struck up a conversation about music, and, specifically, songwriting. Billie Joe had already picked up a guitar and Mike had learned to play music by ear on the family piano and had an interest in jazz. When Mike showed up for a school talent contest with a secondhand bass, the friendship was a done deal. "At first, I played guitar. But one day my friend's brother told me that no matter how many guitar players there are in a band, there's only one bass player. And I was like, 'Bingo!'" Mike told *Bass Player* magazine in a September 1, 2004 interview. "After that, my mom gave me this old pawnshop bass. It was a total piece of sh*t. It had buttons all over it and two flat-wound strings: *E* and *A*. But the bass made the right sounds, so I could have band practice. Billie and I would just plug into the same amp and play all night. I think we were twelve or thirteen."

Mike's family background had its own share of turmoil. His biological mother was a heroin addict at the time of his birth, and his adoptive parents divorced when he was seven years of age. He was shuttled between parents before settling in with his mother. They were financially challenged and between Mike's sister leaving home at the age of thirteen and his mother remarrying a man with whom Mike decidedly did not get along, it was not the easiest of childhoods. The family structure took an unexpected twist later when Mike was in high school; his mother left and he subsequently became surprisingly close with his stepfather, who died when Mike was seventeen.

Mike, born May 4, 1972, followed in his sister's footsteps and left home at the age of fifteen. He made his own way living in turns in a squat full of punks, in his truck, and eventually in a rented room at his best friend Billie Joe's house. He supported himself working as a cook and managed to struggle through his classes and graduate. "I had to do a lot of thinking for myself," he told *Rolling Stone* in its December 28, 1995 issue. "I was one of those kids who'd walk around the neighborhood and talk to the adults and learn a lot. I'm good with people."

When Billie Joe was a freshman at Pinole Valley High his mother procured a 12-string acoustic guitar for her son, "from a guy who specialized in finding illegal instruments—stolen goods, as they say," as he remembered during a 2005 *Guitar World* interview. By the time they were both fourteen, the two fast friends decided it was time to form a band, aptly named Sweet Children. The fledgling band's many influences included the Replacements and local punk heroes Operation Ivy.

Billie Joe opted to drop out of high school, just as his own mother had years ago. His decision was not met with guidance counselors clambering to convince him to reconsider; in fact, he recalls handing his dropout papers to one of his teachers only to be asked, "Who are you?" He and Mike took up residence in an Oakland squat. Billie Joe would years later memorialize that pivotal time period in the song "Welcome to Paradise." *"Dear Mother can you hear me whining? / It's been three whole weeks since I left your home / The sudden fear has left me trembling / 'Cause now it seems that I am out here on my own."*

The two young independents found a substitute home in the established underground punk scene focused around the side entrance to a wicker caning operation: 924 Gilman Street, the punk rock Mecca. This unassuming doorway opened to a microcosm of antics, attitude, and music: The Gilman Street Project. The club was open to all ages,

run by volunteers, unlicensed to sell alcohol, and had been attracting the punk-minded ever since its inception. The non-profit organization aimed to offer up a violence-free environment that would foster creativity.

"That place and that culture saved my life," Billie Joe told *Rolling Stone* in its January 25, 1995 issue. "It was like a gathering of outcasts and freaks. It wasn't about people moshing in a pit and taking their shirt off. That's one thing I hate about the new mainstream thing: Blatant violence. . .To me, punk rock was about being silly, bringing a carpet to Gilman Street and rolling your friends up in it, and spinning it in circles. Or having a pit with people on tricycles or Big Wheels. The whole thing had a serious message to people, but at the same time it was silly and people weren't afraid to talk about love."

The seemingly never-ending stream of punk bands and fans that turned up to playing the cramped, graffiti-covered interior of the club spilled outside onto the street to indulge in a swig of beer—or, if they lacked the funds or the fake ID—a gulp of cough syrup. Billie Joe has often cited speed as a popular drug in the punk scene and although all the band members have been candid about past drug use, they have not ended up in the all-too-common rock-star rehab cycle. "We got over that a long time ago," Mike told *Stuff* magazine in its October 2004 issue. "I don't suggest that for anybody. . .I don't advise anyone [to do drugs]."

Billie Joe and Mike recruited drummer John Kiffmeyer (also known as Al Sobrante, in tongue-in-cheek homage to his hometown, El Sobrante) who had been playing with a band called Isocracy to form a proper band formally christened Sweet Children. In 1988 the rookie group began playing live,

taking on any gig they could lasso with an enthusiasm that far outweighed the sizes of their audiences. The band's very first gig was at Rod's Hickory Pit, where Billie Joe's mother worked as a waitress. Another standout was a high-school party at which they played along with another local band, The Lookouts. Their drummer, Tré Cool, was destined to take over for Al as one-third of Green Day. The opportunity to perform didn't sound too shabby, until it came to light that there *was* no light due to a distinct lack of electricity in the venue—a remote house in the mountains—and the bands had to rely upon candlelight and a generator. Madison Square Garden it wasn't, and there were only a handful of kids to make up the audience, but Billie Joe, Mike, and Al gave it their all. Lawrence Livermore, frontman of The Lookouts and someone else who would play an important role in the future of Green Day, recalled that Sweet Children "played to those five kids as if they were The Beatles at Shea Stadium. It was only their third or forth show ever, but I said right then that I was going to make a record with these guys." Livermore was to repeat these sentiments to *Entertainment Weekly* at the end of the year Green Day hit the big time in the magazine's December 23, 1994 issue, recalling, "The very first time I saw them, they played in a house for about five people, and they had that early-'60s, British Invasion kind of energy. It was just really bright and sparkly."

Bright and sparkly is all very well, but early gigs were often shut down due to noise complaints—don't forget, some of the "venues" weren't much more than someone's basement—but Green Day always had an acoustic guitar up its collective sleeve so that the show could go on. How punk is that? MTV *Unplugged* had nothing on these guys.

Meanwhile, Billie Joe and Mike had become loyal fixtures on the punk circuit, alternately as one of the bands on a club's long bill or as part of the crowd whenever they could scrape together enough money to get in. Sweet Children played a handful of gigs at Gilman Street, the first two in November 1988 and January 1989. On February 11, 1989, Sweet Children shared the Saturday night bill with the Mr. T. Experience, Crimpshrine, and the Well-Hung Monks, and on the 24th they played along with a local band called Sweet Baby. The band's last gig at Gilman under the name Sweet Children was on April Fool's Day, 1989.

LOOK OUT!

Yes, Sweet Children outgrew its name and in April of 1989 the trio rechristened themselves Green Day. The band's new moniker was, in fact, local slang for a day spent smoking pot. Lawrence Livermore, who was making good on his word and just about to release the band's first EP, wasn't particularly amused. Here he had a band known as Sweet Children who had built up a bit of a local reputation, and they wanted him to put out their first record under another name! He acquiesced, however, and in April released a seven-inch pale-green vinyl Green Day EP entitled *1,000 Hours* on his record label Lookout! Records. The four songs, "1,000 Hours" (*Let my hands flow through your hair / Moving closer a kiss we'll share*), "Dry Ice" (*I woke up in a cold sweat / Wishing she was by my side*), "Only of You" (*The first time I caught a glimpse of you / Then all my thoughts were only of you*), and "The One I Want" (*This love is forever / You make my life seem so unreal*) all had in common the subject matter of love, girls, girls, and love. The EP was recorded with an alleged $650 budget in two days. Its cover artwork was a plain pale green type-only cover, but the back cover featured a photo of the Green Day three: Billie Joe sporting long hair and a backwards baseball cap, Al/John hanging loose in surfer shorts, and Mike hanging upside-down from a stair rail. Billie Joe is credited as "Billy." The EP was pressed in a punk-rock rainbow of colors, firstly, of course, green and then purple, red, blue, clear, and yellow.

Green Day continued to play any and every gig they could. Their first Gilman Street show under their new name on May 28, 1989 was a momentous occasion, as it was Operation Ivy's last show. Green Day began appearing on the Gilman Street calendar on a monthly—and sometimes twice-monthly—basis. More and more local gigs came their way. In June of 1989 they played once again on the same bill as The Lookouts, but this time to a more respectable audience of 1,300 at Garberville, California's Veterans Hall. The three bandmates worked at odd jobs and played the odd gig as stand-ins for other bands missing a player in order to earn the necessary cash to subsidize Green Day. They even went back to school—for a joint spring 1990 concert with another local band, Separate Ways, at Billie Joe and Mike's alma mater, Pinole Valley High. "In the early days we just wanted people to listen to our songs. That was all the success we were looking for," Billie Joe told the *Glasgow Sunday Mail* on June 9, 2002.

Lookout! Records and Green Day decided it was about time to put out a full-length album. On December 29, 1989, they commenced what was to be a twenty-two-hour, $600 session and laid down a ten-track album called *39/Smooth*. It was released in 1990. Billie Joe's lyrics were becoming a bit more intricate and mature, and although girls still played a part in the subject matter (see "At the Library" and "The Judge's Daughter"), his signature dark side was already quite evident. Self-doubt, despair, and regret are entrenched in the words sung at punk-rock speed. The song "16" hankers after lost youth and anguishes over the pressures of growing older. In "Road to Acceptance" the young punk wrestles with the issue of self-image and self-confidence, singing, *"I always waste my time just wondering / What the next man thinks of me / I'll never do exactly what I want / And I'll sculpt my life for your acceptance."* In honor of the band's own name, the album also features a little ditty called "Green Day" whose lyrics address—you guessed it—smoking pot. *"My lungs comfort me with joy."* Hey, what do you expect? The guy was only a teenager.

The young trio then recorded a four-song EP in a few hours during an April 20, 1990 session in San Francisco's Art of Ears studio with Andy Ernst, a producer/engineer who specialized in the punk scene including the Swingin' Utters, the Nerve Agents, and Rancid. They called it *Slappy*. *Slappy's* cover artwork showcased a close-up of a panting dog's mug. Three Green Day original tracks, "Paper Lanterns," "Why Do You Want Him?" and "409 In Your Coffee Maker" are followed by a cover of Operation Ivy's "Knowledge." Billie Joe is credited for all lyrics on the three Green Day songs. Once again, the seven-inch vinyl was available in a host of colors, and, once again, the first run was, of course, in green.

Lookout! later smacked *1,000 Hours, 39/Smooth,* and *Slappy* together into one big happy album and released the combination under the name *1,039/Smoothed Out Slappy Hours*. The album, still available today, also features a nineteenth track, "I Want to Be Alone," which was on a Flipside compilation entitled, *The Big One*. *Launch's* review of *1,039/Smoothed Out Slappy Hours* dismissed it as "snotty but revved-up young punks trying to write a decent tune—and mostly falling short," but for such early efforts, the tracks certainly show the seeds of what was to become some top-notch songwriting.

With two EPs and an album under their collective belt, the trio decided it was time to spread the Green Day word a little further a field, and they set off on what was to be the first of many U.S. tours. Tagging along as a roadie was Aaron Cometbus, a future member of Pinhead Gunpowder, one of Billie Joe's ongoing side projects. At one fateful stop on the cross-country trek, Billie Joe met a girl who would years later become his wife: Mankato, Minnesota's Adrienne Nesser, one of a dozen or so audience members.

Whilst in Minneapolis-St. Paul around the Fourth of July 1990, Green Day spent a few spare hours recording a four-song EP of older material on a local label, Skene! Records. The seven-inch vinyl was comprised of four tracks: "Sweet Children," "Best Thing in Town," "Strangeland," and a cover of The

Who's "My Generation." The label pressed 1,500 black and pink vinyl copies on its first pressing with a black-and-white photo of a mike stand and Mike's feet as its cover artwork. A second run of just 600 black-only vinyl copies features different artwork: A black-and-white shot of a broken-down Volkswagen Bug with the caption, "What do you think Mike. . ." An alleged third pressing is also out there. The second pressing featured a handwritten insert headed, "Not a lyric sheet so don't get your hopes up." This extremely rare release—in whichever incarnation—is now highly collectible. There remain rumors and confusion about this release as having been recorded under the name Sweet Children in the late Eighties, but it is indeed a Green Day release entitled *Sweet Children.*

The band wound up their first road trip and returned to their home turf at the end of the summer. Al decided to further his education and while he was away at college in Arcata, California, Billie Joe and Mike enlisted the help of former Lookouts drummer, Tré Cool. As luck would have it, Tré was available, as The Lookouts had reluctantly disbanded in July.

Tré Cool was born Frank Edwin Wright III. His father, who was a helicopter pilot in Vietnam, opted upon his return to move his family to a truly out-of-the-way hiding place: Willits, California, a rural outpost in the Mendocino mountains. It was a good two hours drive down to Berkeley and young Frank spent his youth in virtual isolation, particularly once his sister moved out at the age of eighteen. Fate, however, worked its whacky ways and would have it that the family's "next door" neighbor—a mere mile away—was one Lawrence Livermore, punk rock bandleader of an outfit called The Lookouts. Livermore was also a writer for the infamous San Francisco punk rock bible *MaximumRockNRoll,* and founder-to-be of indie label, Lookout! Records. What on earth he was doing out in the middle of nowhere is anyone's guess, but when the thirtysomething Livermore found himself in need of a drummer for The Lookouts, he, um, naturally looked no further than the twelve-year-old son of his neighbors. The boy played violin. . .not the drums. Mountain jam sessions, over the course of which Frank III was hesitantly entrusted with cymbals one at a time, soon proved that the little punk had what it took. Lest we forget: This was just a kid. "No doubt we embarrassed ourselves many times while we were struggling to master our instruments and figure out what it meant to be in a band, but we were too dumb and too sincere to know it. We just kept on bashing away and howling at the moon," Livermore said. Frank's ever-improving chops were earning him fans further a field than next door. The local high-school band teacher began poaching the young drummer when he was in the sixth grade, actually driving to his rather dilapidated home to pick him up to join in with the big kids as he was the only student of any age who could play jazz.

Frank was duly baptized Tré Cool, became a full-fledged member of The Lookouts, and began making the trek down to Berkeley. He stayed in the vacant bedroom of Dave Dictor, militant punk group MDC's notorious frontman, while MDC was off touring. He reveled in the culture and all of the new people he was meeting every day—it was a hell of a change from the mountains. "I've got my education through punk rock," Tré declared in *The Big Cheese's* October 2004 issue. "It may not be the biggest education in the world but I formed opinions and views on the world and society, feminism and racism through it. I think it changes individuals." A gig with the Canadian band, No Means No, was a major inspiration for the young up-and-comer as he watched the band's tight drummer in awe. Tré still today listens to No Means No's album, *Wrong*, for a bit of nostalgic inspiration. The Lookouts began playing at Gilman Street just weeks after it opened and became a vital part of its scene. Such positive early experiences convinced Tré that punk rock was where he was meant to be. He carried on with conventional education, however, attending community college and taking music-related classes exclusively—jazz ensemble, piano lessons, music theory, music history, classical band—it didn't matter, as long as the subject matter concerned music.

"The first time I ever saw Tré was when I went to see The Lookouts and I was outside drinking with these girls," Billie Joe reminisced to *Kerrang* magazine in its September 2004 issue. "And Tré walked by wearing a weird, old man's plaid suit—none of which was color-coordinated whatsoever—and an

old bathing cap. These girls were like, 'Oh, The Lookouts!' and Tré just kind of turned to them and bowed. I remember thinking that was pretty cool."

It soon became apparent that Tré was the man and that Green Day was now truly the band it was meant to be. The new drummer was in like Flynn and Al graciously accepted the situation and remained in touch with his former bandmates. He went on to play with a few other bands, including a stint with the Ne'er Do Wells.

The new lineup took a courageous step and left their local scene behind in order to embark on a grueling three-month, sixty-four date European tour. They were firmly entrenched in the smoking rows of a long transatlantic flight in November of 1990 and wouldn't see U.S. shores until February 1991. The completely unknown punk trio from California found themselves playing in far from illustrious venues—out-of-the-way pubs all over England and squats in Germany—to crowds of anywhere from twenty to 150 people. The bandmembers, all still teenagers, smuggled their own CDs overseas to sell at gigs. "There were five bands on the bill, four of which sounded like Napalm Death. Then there was us," Billie Joe years later recalled to *NME* in its February 19, 2005 issue. Despite, or perhaps in spite of, their European anonymity, Green Day gave it their all and Billie Joe's swagger was as omnipresent as his beat-up Stratocaster and the tie hanging over his bare chest. The German gigs remain etched in the trio's minds as some of the hardest, and yet best, of times. Never mind that they didn't even have their own equipment and thus were forced to beg and borrow gear for every show. "It made us a really good band, playing on different equipment and in different situations. I think it made us better because obviously there's a language difference and it meant we had to be more animated and project a bit more physically," Billie Joe told *Rock Sound* in its March 2005 issue. "We seemed to get a good response because we were so different from most of the bands playing." Yes, it was tough going, and yes, Billie Joe ended up with head lice, but the tour cemented the band's resolve and solidarity.

More determined than ever after their European adventures, the three bandmates spent the remainder of 1991 getting down to business. In a bookmobile. Yes, that's right: A former mobile library had been forced into an unlikely reincarnation as a tour bus of sorts by Tré's dad, Frank Wright II. In true punk do-it-yourself style, Cool Senior bought the used bookmobile and kitted it out with homemade equipment racks and sleeping bunks. He even went so far as to install himself behind the wheel. Tré's mother Linda explained the punk parental support to *People* magazine in its March 20, 1995 issue recalling, "We always fretted when they went far from home. Frank wanted to be sure they had a good driver." Of course not everyone immediately recognized the Green Day mobile as a punk vehicle. "We had one lady walk into the bookmobile," Mike reminisced to *Stuff* magazine in its October 2004 issue. "We were smoking so much weed. Back then, we just smoked pot all the time. It was pretty funny. She walks in, and she's standing there for a second. She looks and goes, 'Oh! This isn't a bookmobile, is it?' She got all the way into the vehicle in a cloud of smoke." They played gigs all over the local area in addition to their regular Gilman Street appearances and word of mouth was garnering the punk trio audiences that required more than one hand to count.

KERPLUNKED

Billie Joe, meanwhile, had been engaged in a bit of songwriting and the band began working on a host of new material, spending May and September of 1991 back in the Art of Ears studio with Andy Ernst. This time the recording costs came in under $2,000; cost-cutting tactics included Billie Joe and Mike simultaneously belting out the lead and backing vocals.

"I remember after I got back from mastering *Kerplunk*, I put on some headphones and listened to a cassette of it and within about ten seconds of the first song starting, I said to myself, 'Holy sh*t. These guys are going to be massive,'" Laurence Livermore recalled in a *greenday.net* interview.

The album showcased a newly confident Green Day. The new lineup clicked, without a doubt. Tré's tight drum work pulled a drawstring around the band's solidifying style. The very first track, "2,000 Light Years Away," opens with the crash of the new drummer's cymbals and epitomizes all that is Green Day in two minutes and twenty-four seconds. The captivating melody, Mike's grooving bass lines, Billie Joe's now-perfected adenoidal sneer—it's all there. Hell, even the first line of the song is classic *Dookie: "I sit alone in my bedroom / Staring at the walls."* The album careens on, drunkenly and irresistibly catchy, full of hooks and harmonies, coming to a triumphant and sudden halt twelve tracks and a scant thirty-five minutes later.

Kerplunk's cover featured a winking cartoon girl sporting a T-shirt emblazoned with a smiley-faced flower. Sweet. Oh, and she's holding a smoking gun. The liner notes offer a bit of light literary entertainment in the form of a short story entitled, "My Adventure With Green Day" in which an innocent little high-school student named Laurie L. (a nod to Lawrence Livermore) murders her parents in order to go on tour with the band. The delightful little piece was originally written for punk 'zine *Blarg!* Green Day's former drummer in the guise of Al Sobrante is credited as executive producer, and in amongst the many names in the thank-you listing is one Adrienne Nesser.

Lookout! later re-released *Kerplunk* with the *Sweet Children* EP tacked onto the end of the twelve tracks of new material—and you can tell the difference. The other sore thumb on the album is the only tune on the set penned by Tré, "Dominated Love Slave," whose country-western style is oh-so-slightly at odds with the lyric matter (*'Cause I love feelin' dirty / And I love feelin' cheap / And I love it when you hurt me / So drive those staples deep*). All in all, *Kerplunk* was one hell of an album, and Green Day had morphed into one hell of a band.

The punk trio's reputation was spreading via networking with the help of Lookout! Records and underground punk magazines. The band toured steadily throughout 1992. They returned to Germany and the U.K., and also touched down in the Czechoslovakia, Holland, Italy, and Poland. Stateside, the punk trio was racking up an ever-increasing number of gigs. "I remember working in the L.A. clubs, and these bratty kids showed up," Kevin Lyman (who at the time was booking shows and who would go on to found the Warped Tour) told MTV on September 15, 2004. "They had such attitude, but as soon as they played, it was like, 'Anything I can do to help you guys. . .'"

Without much help at all, Green Day was becoming bigger and bigger. From late '91 onwards until the band's final Gilman gig at the end of '93, the now familiar Green Day logo had risen to the top of the punk rock haven's bills. The Green Day three were highly visible within the punk scene. The jury is still out as to whether or not Tré's early predilection for showing up to gigs in a dress and lipstick added to or detracted from the band's notoriety, but there was no doubt that Green Day was becoming too big for its punk-rock britches. The burgeoning band was forced to cancel more than one gig due to far too many fans turning up, as crowds were now numbering in the thousands. The band gradually came to the realization that something had to be done. Things were getting out of control. They needed help, and a support system stronger and further reaching than Berkeley or Lookout! could offer.

It was thus that Billie Joe, Mike, and Tré came to meet with management company Cahn & Saltzman, who would go on to manage the Offspring, Pennywise, Rancid, and other punk acts. Elliot Cahn told *Crossroads* magazine that Green Day's "reputation was that they would have nothing to do with anyone in the music business. . .I think more than being antagonistic, they were cautious and worried. I don't think they wanted a bunch of cigar chewers." The two attorneys apparently left their cigars at home and made a good impression on the punk trio, and hands were shook. Cahn & Saltzman got straight to work, pitching the SoCal punk outfit to all of the major record labels. A&R men began cropping up at sold-out and packed-out Green Day concerts all over the country.

In April of 1993 Green Day took the big step and signed with Reprise Records (Warner Brothers). It was not a decision made lightly. "The whole thought of going on to a huge corporation bothered us, but we're comfortable with it now," Billie Joe told *Billboard* in its April 9, 1994 issue. "Punk isn't really made for the masses, and since we have a strong punk background, we thought that our following would be like, 'What the hell?'" In fact, some of the band's fans asked just that question and weren't exactly thrilled.

The split with Lookout!, however, was amicable and Green Day made sure that their contract with Reprise left all the rights to the band's early material firmly with Lookout! Records. This would prove to be a generous move, as sales of *Kerplunk* and its predecessor would in the future fund a much-expanded Lookout! operation and aid in the advancement of many up-and-coming punk outfits.

Rob Cavallo (son of Bob Cavallo, famed manager of the likes of Prince, Lovin' Spoonful, Paula Abdul, and Alanis Morissette) was the A&R representative for Reprise who made it all come together. "I heard The Beatles in their music, and early '60s Mersey Beat, and the English punk sound," he told *USA Today* in a January 20, 1995 article. "It has a fun, expressive, high-energy power. It's very youthful and exuberant, but angry at the same time. I thought, 'There's gotta be at least 100,000 cool people who will get it.' I had no idea it would snowball." He echoed his instant enthusiasm for the band to *People* magazine in its March 20, 1995 issue. "They have all the elements. Great lyrics, great melodies, interesting influences—the Sex Pistols, the Clash, the Kinks, The Beatles."

The sudden passing on of responsibility to a team of big-time music-industry professionals might have freaked out any other band, but Green Day had been their own manager, bookers, and roadies for far too long. "From the start, we said let's make a concerted effort to stay around for a long time," Tré told the *Associated Press* on February 2, 2005. "Don't make dated records, don't try to strike while the iron is hot and all that. Do what's right for the band long-term. Because we're not going to get sick of doing this—and we knew that ten years ago." Rob Cavallo remembered the early days in a *TAXI* interview, saying, "I'll never forget when Green Day said to me—it was so cool—they said, 'We're going to be a great band.' And they knew it. 'We're going to be a great band no matter what Reprise does for us.'" The years of experience the band had under their collective belt had given them a confidence not often found when the ink's still wet on a major-label record contract. They weren't about to let anything get out of hand unless they wanted it to. And as it turned out, that's exactly what was about to happen.

Green Day hit the studio with that very same Rob Cavallo as co-producer. As Tré told *Drum!* magazine in its December 2004/January 2005 issue, "We always loved Rob, and he always 'got' us as a band. He's sort of like the fourth member." The team set out to mix a new album in a dry, no-reverb style reminiscent of the Sex Pistols. It didn't work. Green Day set off on a two-month tour with Bad Religion in June, but admitted to one another after listening sessions of the "final" mix of their first major-label album that it just didn't sound right. They thought long and hard, reminding themselves that they hadn't used up their entire recording budget, and called Rob Cavallo from the road. He was vastly relieved that the band wasn't happy with the mix, because he wasn't either; they agreed that they would have to reconvene and remix what was to become *Dookie*.

"That's one of the most exciting things I can do in life—to be in the studio with the band and have creative ideas start to flow and to actually be working and getting great stuff on tape," Rob told *TAXI*. "It happened a lot when we were making *Dookie*—no doubt about it. I feel really blessed that I got to make that record with them. Right from getting the drum sound, everything seemed to click. We always knew it. Every time we had a take that was the right take, it was like Tré would throw his sticks and you would always hear them click hitting the floor—and then we would take a break."

"I honestly wanted it to be one of the biggest records of all time because I couldn't see any middle ground," Billie Joe told VH-1 on May 16, 2002. "There's something about mediocrity that I don't want anything to do with. I wanted it to be a splash or else just get overlooked and let people think that there's this cool missing record that only cool people dug. But to go out there and have half a hit, that's more of a kiss of death than being shelved."

The end of December 1993 saw Green Day's farewell Gilman Street gig. They played under another name on a joint bill with Brent's TV. "Almost everyone knew each other and knew all the words to all the songs by both bands," Laurence Livermore said in a *greenday.net* interview. "So we were all dancing and singing along together, and it was all warm and festive and family-like, but there was also this bittersweet feeling that came from knowing that things would never be like this again, that this was the last time we'd all be together this way."

PARADISE BLAST

Dookie was released in February 1994, debuting on the *Billboard* album charts at Number 127 and at an amazing Number One on the Heatseekers chart. "Proudly obnoxious and aggressively immature, punk's noisiest splash since the Clash," declared *USA Today*. Reprise decided to service both the single, "Longview," and its video on the album's street date of February 1 rather than ahead of time in order to maximize impact. It worked. Retailers, radio programmers, and press were sent advance CDs in December 2003, and college radio stations received limited-edition green vinyl copies of *Dookie* in January. Both modern rock radio and college stations immediately began airing "Longview" with a mother's devotion.

In its May 19, 1994 issue, *Rolling Stone* published a picture of a seemingly dumbfounded Billie Joe and band, noting that "Beavis and Butt-head have started a band: It's called Green Day." Although the rather rude query "why bother?" turned up in more than a few early reviews of *Dookie* and the so-called punk revival, as any American teenager could tell you, there is plenty to rebel against without leaving the confines of your average suburban living room. The Sex Pistols went after the Queen; Green Day was pissed off because there was nothing good on TV.

Nothing good, that is, until MTV got its hands on the "Longview" video, produced by Mark Kohr and shot in the band's basement abode in a Victorian house at the corner of Ashby and Telegraph Avenue in Berkeley. The house, overrun with too many people and not enough beds, featured decorative touches such as a Sea Monkeys tank perched on the windowsill, a giant bong lurking in the corner, and a Twister game on the wall; it wasn't your typical MTV backdrop. The clip was added to the music channel's all-important playlist on February 22. By March 28, it was firmly ensconced in the Buzz Bin and there was no going back. Young music fans across the country were entranced with the ultra do-it-yourself band. Most had never heard music like this, and most definitely hadn't seen anyone like Billie Joe Armstrong. The alternately lethargic couch potato / manic twitching punk rocker with a sneering delivery that was part Johnny Rotten, part Elvis was spellbinding. From the opening of the song with its rolling drums and irresistible bass line to the frenetic live performance shots of the trio crammed into the bathroom to Billie Joe's couch-shredding finale, the video was riveting. Before anyone knew what had hit them, Green Day's first single had millions of young Americans singing along to the line *"I'm so bored I'm going blind and I smell like sh*t."* Here was a band that was obnoxious, loud, fast, rude, silly, didn't look like everyone you knew, and didn't look like your parents. Look out people: Green Day had arrived.

As soon as new fans picked up the hot new album—already labeled "pop-punk" by the media—they discovered that Green Day was no one-hit wonder. Every one of the fourteen tracks was a gem, and thirty-nine minutes after hitting play the only sane thing to do was to listen to the whole damn thing again. *Dookie* was addictive. Who would have guessed that an album full of songs about boredom, laziness, masturbation, weed, whining, and self-hatred could be so, well, *catchy?*

When working on what was to become *Dookie*, Billie Joe's songwriting became a bit more circumspect. Rather than coming up with guitar riffs and writing from the guitar, he began composing songs in his head: "The older you get, you become more ambitious, but you also become more self-conscious. So I was writing in secret a little bit more. . .I had no audience at first, but when people actually started showing up to Green Day gigs and buying our records, there was more pressure and more criticism. So I ended up doing it in my world a little bit more," he told *Guitar World* in its

February/March 2005 issue. Living on Tré's couch in the basement of their Ashby Street digs might not seem a creative hotbed, but Billie Joe had plenty of inner inspiration, as well as some real subject matter in the form of his girlfriend, a Berkeley college student who lived upstairs with whom he struck up a year-long relationship. The songs "Sassafras Roots" and "She" are both in part about this girl, with whom Billie Joe abruptly split when she, well, split for a semester abroad in Ecuador. He set off on tour.

Reprise honored Green Day's long-standing tradition of pressing vinyl versions in collectible colors and the *Dookie* LP was available in black, dark green, light green, pink, "rainbow marble," and "baby blue marble."

The chaotic comic strip of a cover was courtesy of Richie Bucher, a local artist and musician who had caught Billie Joe's eye when he illustrated a cover for a band Billie Joe liked called Raool. "I wanted the artwork to look really different. I wanted it to represent the East Bay and where we come from, because there's a lot of artists in the East Bay scene that are just as important as the music," Billie Joe told VH-1 on June 17, 2002. "There's pieces of us buried on the album cover. There's one guy with his camera up in the air taking a picture with a beard. He's this guy Murray that's been around the scene for a long time. He took pictures of bands every weekend at Gilman's. . .the graffiti reading "Twisted Dog Sisters" refers to these two girls from Berkeley. They're punk-rock girls that have been around for years. . .There's a ton of weird little references and inside jokes all over that record."

Despite the unexpected popularity of *Dookie*'s first single, Green Day didn't sit back and enjoy. They got the hell out of the house and hit the road. "The most important ingredient to their success is really their touring base," Warner Brothers/Reprise product manager Geoffrey Weiss told *Billboard* in its April 9, 1994 issue. "They've been out there working their butts off. The second piece of the puzzle is radio and video." The band also made appearances in March on the Jon Stewart Show, Conan O'Brien, and MTV's 120 Minutes.

Green Day set off on a nationwide tour with chosen support band Pansy Division, a self-confessed "queercore" outfit whose song "Rock & Roll Queer Boy" probably wasn't written with stadium audiences in mind. Pansy Division frontman Jon Ginoli described Green Day's approach to *Entertainment Weekly* in its December 23, 1994 edition as, "'We're not going to placate these mainstream people, so we're going to get Pansy Division to wake people up.'" Billie Joe explained to the *Advocate* that the Bay Area and the punk scene in general is supportive of gay rights, saying in the U.S. gay and lesbian newsmagazine's November 23, 2004 issue, "It's all about the alternative lifestyle. Punk rock was about being an individual and coming to your own conclusions." In fact, Gilman Street's credo states, "We will not book or support racist, sexist/misogynist, or homophobic bands or performances." He also spoke of his gay uncle, saying, "He was part of my family from the time I was born. It never even occurred to me that [being gay] was something that was supposed to be offensive."

ICM (International Creative Management) was the booking agency at the helm of Green Day's touring strategy, but the band was instrumental in the conception of keeping ticket prices very low in order to sell out large venues and thereby build their fan base. Instead of a Pearl Jam-style refusal to use Ticketmaster, the band worked with the massive ticketing agent and devised a way to keep tickets between $7.50 and $15.00. A powerhouse in the industry, ICM was responsible for booking some

150 acts, from Faith No More to Dolly Parton, but they were still open to adopting a new plan of attack for Green Day. "We're right at a point of learning something, I think, with this Green Day tour," Bill Elson, head of ICM's music division, told *Billboard* on October 29, 1994. "Prior to Green Day kind of breaking the arena barrier, there haven't been a lot of the newer alternative acts that have been able to put 10,000 people in a building." Green Day helped to keep ticket prices around the price of going to the movies by utilizing a bare-bones road crew. They also demanded lower merchandise pricing and general admission rather than assigned seating whenever possible. Sleeping on the tour bus rather than stopping at posh hotels seemed a small sacrifice in order to keep their gigs within financial reach of their growing legion of young fans. Stormy Shepherd, a player in the underground punk scene ever since launching her booking agency Leave Home Booking from her parents' basement as a teenager, called Green Day's stratagem "a brilliant move" in a March 11, 1995 *Billboard* article. "Who's not going to go for $7.50? It's a whole different way of thinking. It's not about high ticket prices and walking away with a lot of money." Of course, Green Day were never in it for the money, nor did they ever expect to make any.

At the end of April, Green Day left the U.S. for foreign shores for a forty-date European tour that kicked off and rounded up in London. The band brought their trademark brand of Bay Area punk to audiences in Belgium, Denmark, Holland, Italy, Spain, and Sweden. They also found themselves back in Germany, the country that had taught them the ropes right at the beginning. This time around, however, they weren't playing in squats and the chances of catching head lice were considerably diminished. Green Day played nine arenas as support to German punk rock outfit Die Toten Hosen in front of 10,000-strong crowds every night. Beats the hell out of a handful of squatters. The closing gig of the Eurotour was a triumphant gig at London's Astoria II, a great indication of the strong support Green Day was to receive in the U.K. in future years. They returned to America in June to play a host of radio-station gigs, including the high-profile Los Angeles station KROQ's Second Annual Weenie Roast.

At the beginning of the summer of 2004, *Dookie* had achieved Gold status with sales exceeding 500,000 copies. "It's not like we ever aspired to be where we're at right now, but this is where we ended up," Mike told *Entertainment Weekly* in its June 10, 2004 issue. The guys hunkered down and just kept touring. "It's not happening too fast for us to handle," Tré insisted in an interview with the *St. Louis Post-Dispatch* on July 14, 1994. "But the shows are getting pretty crazy. Like we'll sell out places that we never thought we'd even play." The snowball effect was well underway when the band set off on the second leg of the high profile Lollapalooza summer tour, joining the ranks of the big boys, headliners the Beastie Boys and Smashing Pumpkins. Little old Green Day was booked as the opening act, seeing as this was their first big-time tour slot. Their rapidly mushrooming popularity, however, didn't quite suit a noon kick-off and fans stormed the venues' entrance turnstiles to get to the Green Day set in time. "You have to remember that we were not used to playing shows on this scale, and to see the reaction—people jumping seats, people going crazy—every day was just insane," Mike recalled in *Kerrang's* September 2004 issue. "It was like, 'Whoa, it looks like something's happening to our band!'" You could say that again.

LONGVIEW

What do most young guys on the verge of rock stardom do? Settle down and get married, right? Not. But that's exactly what Billie Joe decided to do right in the midst of the *Dookie* madness. In July 1994, he married girlfriend Adrienne Nesser. When Billie Joe met his wife-to-be during Green Day's first tour, the two hit it off, but lost touch for a year or so during which time Billie Joe was busy writing *Dookie* and Adrienne became engaged to someone else. Eventually, however, they rekindled their initial spark and Adrienne moved out to California. Their wedding was a quiet backyard affair. Billie Joe's remembrance of the event to *Rolling Stone* in its January 26, 1995 issue was characteristically frank. "I was really nervous, so I started pounding beers and so did Adrienne. The ceremony lasted five minutes. Neither of us are any religion, so we pieced together speeches. One Catholic, one Protestant, one Jewish. It was a lot of fun. Then we went to the Claremont Hotel, and we f***ed like bunnies." What a romantic! A full decade later he told *Alternative Press* in its October 2004 issue, "I couldn't believe it when we first got married—it was one of those things where you're like, 'Hey! I've got a crazy idea! Let's get hitched and we'll do it in the backyard!' Her parents never knew me or anything like that, so it was just this kinda strange, wild thing that we did. Looking back ten years later, on how it's evolved, it's definitely had its ups and downs. But Adrienne is truly one of the sweetest people on the planet." The very next day the newlyweds discovered, to their absolute delight, that Adrienne was pregnant and that they were to be parents.

Billie Joe and Adrienne bought a house in North Berkeley before the baby was born. Fans began showing up in the yard in droves after one such "fan" announced the Armstrong family's address on local radio. Billie Joe, suitably pissed off, was forced to sell his first home and move elsewhere in his first bout with one of the battles of fame—safeguarding your privacy.

Billie Joe was well aware that his decision to get hitched at the cusp of rock 'n' roll fame was unusual. "The funny thing is that I wouldn't want to be in a band if I wasn't doing it with the family," he told

Alternative Press in its June 2002 issue. "It seems like I wouldn't want to buy into the cliché of being a rock star and having chicks and drugs around me. For me, the fact that I can share it with somebody is a lot better than doing it alone." He echoed these sentiments in the November 26, 2004 issue of London's *Mirror,* saying, "My parents split up when I was young so I know what that's like. I don't aim to repeat the pattern. Getting married was a wild thing we decided to do overnight, but the reason we did it still remains the same. Adrienne's one of the sweetest people on the planet. Of course there have been temptations on the road, that's just the way it is in a rock band. But what we have is far too valuable to ever do anything to harm it."

That little matter of marriage taken care of, the twenty-fifth anniversary of the legendary Woodstock festival was the next event on the horizon. Woodstock II was held August 13 and 14 in Saugerties, New York on an 840-acre site. Some 250,000 tickets were sold at the premium rate of $135 a shot, but reportedly thousands of additional music fans made it past the gates, chain-link fencing, and 550 state troopers. Corporate sponsors Pepsi, Haagen-Dazs ice cream, and Apple were on board, and critics labeled the event a jaded cash-in. Mike freely admitted to *Time* magazine on August 22, 1994, that Woodstock "is really corporate. But that's one of the reasons we're playing. It's helping us make up a lot of the money we've lost touring, being out there keeping our ticket prices low." The second time around the bill included Aerosmith; Alice in Chains; Arrested Development; Blind Melon; Blues Traveler; Joe Cocker; the Cranberries; Crosby, Stills & Nash; Sheryl Crow; Cypress Hill; Bob Dylan; Melissa Ethridge; Henry Rollins; James; Metallica; the Neville Brothers; Nine Inch Nails; Porno for Pyros; Red Hot Chili Peppers; Santana; and a hell of a lot of mud due to wet weather.

No one could have forecasted that Green Day's Sunday afternoon south stage set would be remembered as the defining moment of the entire event, but the fans sure were impatient for them to begin. During the extended world-music segment featuring a string of artists from Peter Gabriel's W.O.M.A.D. festival, the crowd periodically booed and chanted for Green Day, forcing an announcement: "Green Day will be on when their turn comes; please give these musicians their turn."

When Green Day finally did take the stage, all hell broke loose. Mud began to fly. The kings of neo-punk fulfilled their royal roles with awe-inspiring gusto, leading the biggest mud fight ever to be documented on film. Billie Joe pulled his pants down (the inspiration behind a scolding letter from the lead singer's very disappointed mother), and Mike's front teeth were shattered by a security guard unable to tell the difference between a mud-covered rock star and a mud-covered fan. The idea that playing loud, fast, pogoing music to a massive, dirty crowd can only be topped by self-exposure and a brawl with your own security goons makes all the sense in the world, but in reality it just plain got out of hand. Billie Joe yelled to the crowd, "This isn't peace—it's f***ing anarchy!" as he attempted to wrestle a sound out of a guitar covered in balls of earth. Mike ended up with three broken teeth and the three bandmembers had to be airlifted out by helicopter. Billie Joe described the anniversary of the renowned peace and love fest as "f***ing psycho" to *Spin* magazine and went on to quote the staggering statistic that there were 750 legs broken at Woodstock II before Green Day went on stage (the post-mud fight numbers aren't in yet). His concise summary of the historical event was, "It was the closest thing to anarchy I've ever seen in my life, and I didn't like it." Nor did manager Elliot Cahn, who himself performed at the original Woodstock as a member of Sha Na Na. He told *Entertainment Weekly* in its August 26, 1994 issue, "I've got a hurt guy in my band, so I gotta say I'm pretty bummed about it." Perhaps he cheered up a bit the week following Woodstock II when *Dookie* shot to Number Five on the charts.

The summer—and what a summer it had been—wound down, but the back-to-school blues were alleviated by the MTV Music Video Awards ceremony held in New York City's Radio City Music Hall. The "Longview" clip was nominated in three categories, and although it didn't win, Green Day definitely triumphed with the most energetic performance of the evening. Kids who had seen the video but had never had the punk pleasure of the live Green Day experience were convinced that the frantic band in the video was for real. The "Longview" music video also garnered three *Billboard* Music Video Awards nominations later in the year in the alternative/ modern rock category up against the likes of Nirvana, the Beastie Boys, Soundgarden, Beck, and the Counting Crows, and this time Green Day won—twice. "Longview" was declared Best New Artist Clip of the Year, and Maximum Vision Clip of the Year, an award created to honor the video that is most effective in advancing an artist's career. Warner Brothers' director of national video promotion, Wendy Griffiths, accepted the New Artist award for the band at the 16th annual award ceremony in Santa Monica, California (Billie Joe, Mike, and Tré had a concert in Dominguez Hills, California, that evening), saying, "This is the first award this band has ever won!" The band was also nominated for Modern Rock Act of the Year at the *Billboard* Music Awards, but bowed to winners Stone Temple Pilots.

But enough with the awards already—more mudslinging was in the cards. The band decided to give Boston fans a free concert on September 9 at the Hatch Shell, and an overwhelming 65,000 turned up for the festivities. Less than half an hour after Billie Joe struck his first chord, city officials pulled the plug as the massive moshing crowd had broken through stage barricades. Needless to say, the sudden halt wasn't well received and the audience refused to go on home quietly despite the continued announcement "Green Day has left the building," and a contingent began hurling beer bottles and mud about. A reported thirty arrests, fifty injuries, and $20,000 worth of damages later, what was surely Green Day's first and last Boston freebie was definitely over.

In October the pond-hopping strategy carried on, with the band returning to Europe for another run, this time for a three-week tour. Meanwhile back at home *39/Smooth* and *Kerplunk* were enjoying a little ancillary spotlight action themselves, with appearances on the *Billboard* Top Pop Catalog Albums chart at Number Twenty-Seven and Number Twenty respectively. Lookout! Record's sales were soaring. "We're a label that relied on word-of-mouth," Chris Appelgren, the indie label's operations director, told *Billboard* on November 5, 1994. "They sold a few thousand every month. That doesn't compare to what they're doing right now. Each month has surpassed the last."

Back in the U.S. after the European run, Green Day returned the favor to Die Toten Hosen, bringing the German band along for the ride as support act to November gigs in Canada, as well as Stateside concerts in December in New York and Philadelphia.

Billie Joe, Mike, and Tré participated in one of the first of what was to be a long list of charity events when they joined a host of artists who worked behind the counters of retail shops all over the country to raise funds to combat AIDs for LIFEbeat's CounterAid on December 3rd. An appearance on *Saturday Night Live* with the band performing a bit of new material in the form of the song "Geek Stink Breath" rounded out the day nicely.

What better place to celebrate an unimaginably successful year than Madison Square Garden? Green Day joined a festive bunch of major acts including Bon Jovi, Sheryl Crow, Hole, Indigo Girls, Toad the Wet Sprocket, and Weezer at the top Manhattan venue's Acoustic Christmas Concert hosted by New York City radio station, Z100, on December 5th. In his usual style, Billie Joe made sure that Green Day's set was a standout—he turned up for the band's 2:00 AM encore performance of "She" stark raving naked, with only his trusty guitar to keep things from getting all-out pornographic. Ah, a little nudity for the holidays warms the punk heart.

By the time 1994 was winding down, *Dookie* had sold well over three million copies in the U.S. and spawned not one, not two, not three, but an incredible four hit singles. "Basket Case," the band's follow up to "Longview," was about "anxiety attacks and feeling like you're ready to go crazy." Billie Joe told

VH-1 on May 16, 2002. "At times I probably was. I've suffered from panic disorders my entire life. I thought I was just losing my mind. The only way I could know what the hell was going on was to write a song about it. It was only years later that I figured out I had a panic disorder." The song's video had the band playing in a mental institution—the treatment complete with Tré hitting the skins in a wheelchair—and was further confirmation that these guys were true entertainers. Billie Joe's blue Stratocaster covered with stickers and emblazoned with the initials B.J. along with his arm-jerking assault on the guitar he called "Blue" were becoming very familiar to MTV viewers. The next two singles up to bat, "When I Come Around" and "Welcome to Paradise," enjoyed an open-armed welcome to the airwaves after the success of *Dookie's* first two singles.

The undeniably, unexpectedly triumphant year was nearly over, and the band that hadn't stopped to take a breath was ready to do just that. "I'm just exhausted," Billie Joe told *Entertainment Weekly* in early December for its December 23, 1994 issue. "Totally. We've outdone ourselves in a serious way. I have insomnia problems anyway, so it's hard for me to sleep. That's the main thing I'm looking forward to: I'll probably sleep for the rest of the year."

It had been quite a year for the music industry. Nirvana's Kurt Cobain, spokesman for the slacker generation, took his own life. Trent Reznor introduced a new kind of electronic fury and annihilated a warehouse-full of keyboards. The Rolling Stones went on tour yet again and The Eagles kissed and made up. Solo women artists—Liz Phair, Tori Amos, Sheryl Crow, Courtney Love, Björk—stood out and spoke out. The flannel shirted kings of Grunge took a bow and when their heads were down, a bunch of punks jumped in and threw them off the stage.

Mike expressed his amazement at it all to *Rolling Stone* in its January 26, 1995 edition, which featured none other than Green Day on its venerable cover. "Someone said to me before a show the other day, 'Fifteen thousand people at this arena—this is everything you ever dreamed of.' I turned to him and said, 'Correction. It's everything I *never* dreamed of.'"

"The first time we were the biggest band on the planet, it kind of happened by accident," Tré reflected in a February 11, 2005 *Entertainment Weekly* article. "We had been told, and it had been proved many times, that you can't sell punk rock and there will never be a big punk rock record," says Cool. "We blew that myth out of the water." Yep, you sure as hell did.

OUT SOLD

Not everyone was delighted with Green Day's massive success. A grunge-weary public and a music industry looking for the next big thing may have welcomed the band with open arms and wallets, but those who knew that punk wasn't shiny and new weren't quite as thrilled with the spotlight. *MaximumRockNRoll* magazine, the Bay Area punk bible, took offense at Green Day's breaking of hardcore rule number one: Don't Sell Out. Selling out, in politically correct punkese, consists of signing with a major label, making loads of money, and becoming MTV darlings while still clinging to the right to call yourself punk. The 'zine featured cover headlines in 1994 such as "Major Labels: Some of Your Friends Are Already This F***ed." Apparently rebelling is only kosher if it doesn't get you anywhere.

Despite its anti-violence stance, Gilman Street, parent and guardian to so many punk rockers, does not take kindly to successful children coming home to visit. Jello Biafra, ex-lead singer for the Dead Kennedys, was severely beaten by members of the crowd there as chants of "Sell Out!" and "Pop Star!" filled the air. Green Day would forever put the punk haven on a pedestal, while accepting that they could never go back.

Billie Joe, Mike, and Tré couldn't help but be affected by the negativity. Being labeled "punk mock" and "Gap punk" by detractors just plain wasn't fair; these guys had definitely paid their punk dues. "A lot of people who don't know anything about where we come from or what punk rock means to us try and decipher it all. You know, it's kind of like talking to a horse about how to cook," Mike said to MTV on October 1, 2000. "There's punks who know where we came from, and then there's the people whose rich parents pay for them to be degenerates," he told *Rolling Stone* in its January 26, 1995 issue. "It's funny how PC people can be when they have money. We got these fliers that said, 'Tell Green Day to F*** Off For Bringing MTV Into Our Scene.' I've never seen one TV in the punk clubs we've played. I think your mother and father need to take your cable away, is what they need to do."

And who says punk has to be played in grimy backstreet clubs? And what's so wrong with a wider audience enjoying good music? "We got a chance to be playing these arenas and I'm really grateful for that," Billie Joe told *Rolling Stone* in its December 28, 1995—January 11, 1996 issue. "I'm not going to sit here and say, 'F*** our fans, man, they're not true Green Day fans because they heard us on MTV.' These people are paying to see me play. A lot of these kids have never heard the kind of music that we play before, and a lot of them are from somewhere where there's a single parent that works their ass off to give them twelve bucks to go out and see us play this show."

Green Day were just doing what they'd been doing for years—except in front of the whole world. Some would insist that giving up most, if not all, of your touring profit to ensure that as many kids get to see the show as possible is pretty damn punk rock. Jim Baltutis of Reprise Records told *Amusement Business* in its January 8, 1996 issue, "I can't speak directly for the band, but they don't

really make any money when they are on the road. I know they actually lost plenty last time they went out because the ticket prices are so low."

In direct contrast to the "sell out" accusations, Green Day really weren't in this for the money. And admirably, considering their never having had enough of the green stuff, they didn't go berserk when they did get a bit. "You see a lot of bands who get their first taste of money—and that's usually an advance; it's not actually their money— and immediately they're buying things like sports cars and other things that they think shows them to be successful," Tré observed to *Kerrang* in its July 2004 issue. "I wasn't like that. I bought the things that I needed, the things I'd never had before. So I got myself somewhere to live, I got myself health insurance." No one can sensibly call that selling out. "We have a lot of money— what are we going to do with it?" Billie Joe asked in a December 23, 1994 *Entertainment Weekly* article. "I don't know. My mother would always ask me, 'What would you like for Christmas?' Nothing. What do I need? I have a pretty low standard of living." Mike concurred. "I set my life up so I could be

happy regardless of what my income was. If you can set up a lifestyle where you can always be happy—mine was around musicians and friends—and have no other expectations, then anything else that happens is icing on the cake," he told *Rolling Stone* in its December 28, 1995 issue. Years down the road, the band's financial philosophy remained intact. "We're not out collecting Ferraris, diamonds, and jewels and stuff. We still practice in the same garage," Tré told the *Denver Rocky Mountain News* on November 28, 1997. "The best part is we can afford nice instruments and we can thrash them. If something has a history to it, I'm not going to thrash it, but if something is nice and new and all pretty, then I'll smash it." Now that's punk rock, not punk mock.

The band hadn't really had a chance to figure it all out. "You sort of adapt. When everything was just exploding and getting big, you're on the road so much you never get a chance to sit around and analyze it. You just keep going and you come back home and then all of a sudden things are different and people look at you funny." Billie Joe said during a May 28, 1998 *Launch* interview. He complained of being pegged as "spokesmen for a new punk generation" to the *Glasgow Sunday Mail* in its January 7, 1996 issue, saying, "I don't see how baring your buttocks or spitting at a crowd is saying anything. There are no pretensions about us. The fans relate to that. Maybe that is the real reason we are so popular."

Nonetheless, the band wasn't able to fully appreciate their success. "The backlash, our hometown feeling like we sold out, we were playing into that," Billie Joe told *Rolling Stone* in its February 24, 2005 issue. "Ninety-nine percent of it was good, and we were focusing on the one percent that wasn't. That's one thing that I wish we could have changed. Who gives a sh*t?"

WALKING
EQUILIBRIUM

Happy New Year! Green Day's ascension to the Big Time was made official by rock bible *Rolling Stone*. The magazine's January 26, 1995 Annual Music Awards issue's cover featured the punk trio—complete with Billie Joe's full frontal smirk—under the header BEST NEW BAND. The lead singer's genius pullquote sealed the deal: "I never thought that being obnoxious would get me where I am now."

Indeed, it turned out that Billie Joe, like any rock 'n' roll frontman worth his salt, was adept at giving good quote. His flair for smart-ass replies further boosted the band's bratty image. An early list of his most succinct verbal treasures would surely include his summary of sexuality ("People don't know what the f*** they are"), his self-analysis ("I'm an asshole trying to be a nice guy"), and his reply to being designated the voice of his generation: "More like the *butt* of a generation."

And so we hit upon yet another reason for Green Day's huge popularity: They didn't take themselves seriously—it was all about music. Music journalists accustomed to grilling artists about their opinions on everything under the sun except music hit the wall when it came to Green Day. Here were three guys who seemed to have gotten back to the basic reasons for being in a band. Making and playing music, period. They offered no apologies for acting their age. They were rock stars, a chart-topping pop act, and punks all at once. What more do you want?

Year Two of Green Day's takeover of the music scene was, to say the least, eventful. Both Billie Joe and Tré became fathers in the midst of all the madness. Billie Joe and Adrienne named their son Joseph Marciano and called him Joey. Tré and his now-first-ex-wife Lisea named their daughter Ramona. Do I smell a Ramones tribute? "You gotta be a patient motherf***er to have kids," Tré disclosed to *Spin* in its November 2004 issue. "First of all, they take nine months to be ready, and that's f***ed up. And then when they're born, it's like, wow, stress. My first child, I was wondering if she was going to take her next breath, every minute." Billie Joe took fatherhood in his manic stride, approaching parenting at his usual optimum velocity, bragging that he could change a diaper in "thirty seconds—one commercial!" A few years further down the parental road, Billie Joe told the *St. Louis Post-Dispatch* on December 21, 1997, "The thing is, being in this rock 'n' roll world, it's pretty self-absorbed, whereas being a parent is totally selfless. You don't belong to you anymore, you belong to this child you need to stick around for. It's good. It's definitely a balance. On one side, it keeps me grounded. And on the other side, it's fun. He's a cool kid."

The ultimate award in the music industry is the Grammy and Green Day was honored with not one but four nominations in the listing of the 37th Annual Grammys to be held March 1st. *Dookie* won Best Alternative Music Performance, and deservedly so. "Longview" was up for Best Hard Rock Performance, "Basket Case" for Best Rock Performance by a Duo or Group, and the band itself for the highly coveted Best New Artist.

Meanwhile, Green Day continued to quietly engage itself in any charitable causes that came their way, and were only too keen to sign themselves up for two benefit concerts for concerns close to home: May 27th and 28th gigs at the Henry J. Kaiser Auditorium in Oakland, California. Proceeds from the concerts went to the San Francisco Coalition on Homelessness, the Berkeley Free Clinic, the Haight-Ashbury Free Clinic, and Food Not Bombs.

Touring throughout the U.S., the band brought a twelve-person road crew along for the ride. The bookmobile days were far behind them; they now required four trucks and two tour buses. Still a bit shaken by the Woodstock II experience, Green Day were very wise with regard to security and crowd control. The band wanted to be sure that the kids had a great time and didn't get hurt—either by overzealous local security or by each other. Doors to all shows were open a good two hours ahead of time to allow a relaxed entrance. The band's production manager, Mitch Cramer, took a very hands-on approach and always worked the gigs with the venue's own security, meeting with them the day of the show and joining them at the barricades during the concerts. It wasn't unusual for him to jump into the mosh pit if things got dicey. "If you let the kids control where they go and how they go, you are going to have a lot less injuries and problems than if you try to control them," Cramer told *Amusement Business* in its January 8, 1996 issue. "Stopping kids coming over the walls, you're going to have confrontations. That's when kids and/or security are going to get hurt. You've got to let them just come over because the ones that want to be on the floor will get on the floor. If you let them just do it, chances of risking injury are so much slighter."

In July of 1995, select radio stations broke out with a new Green Day single, "J.A.R." The track, recorded for the soundtrack of a less-than-successful film entitled *Angus,* was written in memory of a friend of the band's, Jason Andrew Relva, who died in a car accident. The problem was, the single was not due for release for another few weeks. Rumor had it that the band's management—Cahn & Saltzman—had leaked the song to an elite groups of DJs as a sort of enticement designed to induce them to play new music from the management team's own new label, (510) Records. Shortly there-after Green Day severed their ties with Cahn & Saltzman. Whether the alleged leak was the cause of the break is unclear, but as Billie Joe put it to *Rolling Stone* in the magazine's year-end issue, "We felt like we weren't being treated like people anymore but as assets. And so we were just like, 'F*** this.'" Solving the problem in true punk fashion, the band reverted to the do-it-yourself maxim that hadn't yet let them down and became their own managers.

Releasing a follow-up album to a multi-Platinum smash that brought your band to the forefront of the pop-music scene is a daunting task. Luckily, Green Day weren't known for biding their time. In between touring, the band hit the studio to record another album with Rob Cavallo once again joining them at the helm. They chose Jerry Finn, who had worked his magic on *Dookie,* to mix.

The result was the appropriately titled *Insomniac,* which hit the shelves in October of 1995, debuting at Number Two on the *Billboard* charts while its predecessor still reigned at Number 93 after a solid 87 weeks on the charts. A frantic, freaked out, and tweaked out thirty-three minutes and fourteen tracks later, it was evident that Billie Joe and company weren't the multicolored flash in the pan critics had been claiming. An inexorable assault on the senses, the album was darker and more belligerent than *Dookie.* Billie Joe's lyrics were brutal and filled with self-loathing, and if they weren't enough to cause a lack of sleep, the fast and furious pace of *Insomniac* should do the trick.

Billie Joe weighed in on the album in a September 20, 1997 *Billboard* article, saying, "It did a lot better than I thought it was going to do. We were prepared for what people were going to say. From the sound of it, we knew it wasn't going to sell as much as *Dookie.* . .It had a sort of one-track mind. It was very aggressive through the whole thing. It was relentless. It sold four million worldwide, and that's great. Bands dream of selling that many records." The band was still working through the sell-out backlash when they created the album. Billie Joe looked back on the *Insomniac* days during a November 26, 2001 *Rolling Stone* interview, saying, "We were going through an identity crisis a little bit. We felt like an underground band, but we were a mainstream band so there's that thing we had to deal with. And that's something I wish I could have enjoyed more and kind of say, "F*** it!" a little bit."

Dookie was a hard act to follow—the press was overly fond of the term "sophomore slump"—but *Insomniac* was in fact an outstanding piece of work, and those in the know knew it. *Rolling Stone* awarded the album a major four (out of five) stars in its very positive review, noting, "Without slipping into virtuosity, Billie Joe, bassist Mike Dirnt, and drummer Tré Cool have improved and tightened up their playing." And declaring, "In punk, the good stuff actually unfolds and gains meaning as you listen without sacrificing any of its electric, haywire immediacy. And Green Day are as good as this stuff gets."

Green Day kept up their tradition of creative album covers and this time around the artwork was the work of montage master Winston Smith. The artist was best known within the punk scene for his album covers for Jello Biafra and the Dead Kennedys. Smith had actually gotten involved with the late '70s/early '80s punk-music scene when he began creating posters advertising fictitious gigs for imaginary bands at clubs that didn't exist and plastering them all over San Francisco. He entitled the *Insomniac* piece, "God Told Me to Skin You Alive," a Jello Biafra/Dead Kennedy's reference. Also featured are three skulls—one per band member—and if you fancy a bit of punk rock Where's Waldo, see if you can find the third. (Hint: Hold the artwork flat and look at it from an angle. What appeared to be a bit of wood emanating from the flames turns into a human skull.)

Insomniac delivered its own foursome of singles. The first, "Geek Stink Breath," an ode to a druggie with rotting teeth still managed to maintain Green Day's love affair with melody in the midst of its unpleasant message and had us all singing along to the chorus, *"I'm on a roll / No self control / I'm blowing off steam with / Meth Amphetamine."* The video treatment was a little hard to take, with performance shots intercut with close-ups of a tongue-pierced dental patient undergoing a very bloody tooth removal. Next up was "Stuck With Me" whose MTV clip was a bit easier on the eye, creatively combining black-and-white performance with *Insomniac's* cover art come to life in animation. The third single, "Brain Stew/Jaded," was a radio favorite and a standout track on the album with its AC/DC-style power chords. The end of the dusty junkyard video sees the tagged-on bonus mini-track, "Jaded," receive its own suitably hyperactive treatment.

In 1996, one final single, "Walking Contradiction" hit the air and videowaves. It was the only *Insomniac* single to make a mark on the charts, peaking at Number Nine on the *Billboard* Mainstream Rock Tracks and Number Five on the Modern Rock tracks. The video is a wonderful romp through Green Day land, with the guys strolling through an outer-city neighborhood inadvertently wreaking havoc. The clip earned the band another Grammy nod in the form of a nomination for Best Music Video, Short Form. Up against some mighty strong fellow nominees (Alanis Morissette's "Ironic," Michael Jackson's "Earth Song," Smashing Pumpkins' "Tonight, Tonight," and the winners, some band named The Beatles for their "Free as a Bird" video), the punk rock long shot didn't have much of a chance, but as they all say, it's an honor just to be nominated. Yeah, right.

In March of that year the band received a bit of hometown validation—and maybe an apology of sorts for all those cries of sell out—when Green Day won two Bay Area Music Awards, Outstanding Hard Music Album for *Insomniac* and Outstanding Drummer/Percussionist for our Tré.

The insanity of relentless touring finally took its toll and Green Day were forced to cancel their 1996 European tour due to exhaustion. "That whole period wasn't a great time for us," Billie Joe years later

acknowledged to *Kerrang* in its September 2004 issue. "Everyone in the band was getting panic attacks. We were doing stupid things, like trying to manage ourselves. And when we played live, we were playing way too fast—we had no groove, so that even the shows sounded as if we were trying to get the whole thing over with. And, basically, something had to give."

HITCHIN' A RIOT

Of course, R&R to these three didn't preclude regular "band practice," and the boys had been busy. Green Day hit the studio once again in April of 1997 with their trusted producer Rob Cavallo ready to record their third album, the very same month that Mike became a father when his girlfriend Anastasia gave birth to the couple's daughter, Estelle Desiree. With a whopping thirty-five songs under their collective belt, the pick-and-choose process was underway and rumors of a double album or, at the very least, an album twice as long as its predecessors, abounded. The band had had a good year to write, and it showed. Green Day was to spend a record four months recording this time around—far more time than they had devoted to any album in the past. "I spent a lot of time in the studio while they were recording," Howie Klein, U.S. president of Reprise Records told *Billboard* in its September 20, 1997 issue. "What I realized immediately is that they had seemed to mature in their musical direction. It wasn't just more of the same. There was so much growth in the band."

Green Day broke from the studio to play an unannounced gig at L.A.'s intimate Viper Room on July 19th. The concert was actually a warm-up of sorts in anticipation of the band's appearance at Japan's Mount Fuji Rock Festival at the end of the month. The festival, however, was literally blown off—right in the middle of the Red Hot Chili Peppers' set Hurricane Rosie joined the party and shut the place down on Day One of the weekend concert. The devastation to the entire concert site was so severe that the entire festival was canceled and Green Day never had a chance to hit the stage. They contented themselves with a field trip to a local amusement park along with fellow artists Beck, the Foo Fighters, the Chili Peppers, and the Prodigy before heading back to California and the studio in order to spend the month of August mixing what was to be *Nimrod,* their fifth studio album.

Billie Joe spoke to MTV News on September 2, 1997 from the studio prior to the album's release and defiantly declared, "I don't really give a rat's ass what anybody thinks of this record because I know I like it." He went on to say, "This record, more so than any other record, I think we sort of bled over this one a little more. I mean, this is a record I've been wanting to make since the band pretty much started." Confident words, which would prove to be well founded when the album dropped on October 14th.

Billboard proclaimed on September 20, 1997, "Growth and maturity aren't words one usually associates with punk trio Green Day, but with the release of *Nimrod*. . .those two words are frequently popping up in discussions." *Rolling Stone's* official review awarded the album three-and-a-half stars and asserted, "This music is a long way from

Green Day's apprenticeship at the Gilman Street punk clubs in Berkeley, Calif. But now that the band has seen the world, it's only fitting that Green Day should finally make an album that sounds as if it has." *USA Today* gave the album a very favorable review in its November 4, 1997 issue, declaring Green Day "a band that's surviving growing pains without sacrificing youthful vigor." The album squeaked into the Top Ten with a Number Ten debut on the *Billboard* charts.

Nimrod saw the band go beyond those infamous three chords and featured Billie Joe on harmonica, Tré on bongos and tambourine, That Dog's Petra Haden on violin, No Doubt's horn section on, well, horns, and—wait for it—string arrangements courtesy of Beck's father. No, really. "We really wanted to go down different avenues this time and stretch as much as possible," Billie Joe told MTV on October 13, 1997. "In the past, I think there was a small sense that we were holding back from going in different musical directions. This time we went for it."

"With *Nimrod* we just wanted to prove ourselves as a band, which is what I think we did," Billie Joe told *Kerrang* in its September 2004 issue. "We tried some things that we'd never done before and it came off great. I'm very proud of that album." He did exhibit his sense of humor in a November 7,

1997 interview with the *Virginia Pilot,* saying, "They're just a bunch of stupid little songs. What can you do, go around and tell everyone it's the second coming of Christ? No one wants to hear that. Just play the songs and shut the (blank) up."

The band celebrated the album's release in true New York City-style, complete with music-industry bigwigs, Winona Ryder, and a selection of the city's finest drag queens all crammed into one of downtown's hippest little clubs, Don Hill's, situated on the unfashionable (and, ergo, cool) end of Spring Street. The party took place the very day the album hit the shelves and followed Green Day's kick-ass performance during the afternoon taping of *David Letterman.* An open bar and Don Hill's house band, Squeezebox, kicked off the evening, but as the late-night hours approached, Green Day took the stage and played a raucous set of covers, including songs by none other than Marilyn Manson, Def Leppard, Van Halen, The Who, and Cheap Trick—and, of course, Survivor's "Eye of the Tiger." A few Green Day songs made their way into the mix as well, and the festivities came to a close with Tré and Billie Joe trading instruments in order to send the remaining revelers homeward into the wee hours with a wee country jingle.

Despite (or perhaps in spite of) the press tossing about terms like "mature" to describe the newest Green Day release, the band exhibited some decidedly good old brat-punk behavior at an in-store appearance at New York City's downtown Tower Records store. After the store was filled to capacity with fans and hundreds more were turned away at the door, Billie Joe opened the event with a rather irresponsible salutation, "Let's have a f***ing riot!" He then spray-painted "NIMROD" and "F*** YOU" on the storefront windows and obligingly mooned the crowd outside before launching into a crazed forty-minute set which culminated in the lead singer lobbing Tré's bass drum from the second floor performance area onto the CD racks on the main floor below. Reports of damage to the store varied widely, from hundreds to thousands of dollars worth, but it was clear that Tower wasn't amused. When asked by MTV News on November 12, 1997 if the band would be invited back, the store's manager Hedi Kim responded, "Never," and then added, "They may be in the cut-out bin in the near future anyway." Now, now, no need to be nasty.

To pre-empt any early leaks, Reprise released the album's first single "Hitchin' a Ride" in late August, a good six weeks before *Nimrod* hit the shelves. The new Green Day single didn't disappoint and enjoyed heavy airplay. Once the song's video was handed over to MTV, "Hitchin' a Ride" was well on its way. Directed by Green Day mainstay Mark Kohr, the clip is a sort of traveling circus that suits the song's marching band feel to a "T."

After a quickie promotional excursion in Europe hitting Milan, Vienna, Hamburg, Cologne, Paris, and London, Green Day set out on a U.S. tour booked by Rob Light of Creative Artists Agency. The band was now with Bob Cavallo (Rob's father) and Patrick Magnarella of Atlas/Third Rail Management. Foregoing the arenas this time around the States, the band focused on smaller venues, entertaining anywhere between 1,200 to 3,000 fans per show. The tour began on October 30th in Dallas, Texas and wound down in mid-December with three consecutive dates at The Fillmore in San Francisco. "The whole point of this tour is to be closer to the audience," Billie Joe told the *Atlanta Journal and Constitution* in a November 7, 1997 interview. "It's going to be just the three of us and them in smaller places. Dropping the front and being vulnerable is the main idea behind *Nimrod*."

Green Day joined No Doubt, Scott Weiland, Perry Farrell, Beck, Fiona Apple, and a festive host of other artists in December for KROQ's Almost Acoustic Christmas weekend-long concert in Los Angeles. Billie Joe brought his distinctive brand of holiday cheer to the event by hurling a Christmas tree into the crowd after mooning everyone. Ho ho ho!

After the holiday break, the band set off on a marathon world tour that would take them all over the global shop and all the way into November. Kicking off in Belfast, Ireland, the European leg saw Green Day play twenty-nine dates in the U.K., France, Belgium, Holland, Sweden, Germany, Denmark, the Czech Republic, Slovenia, Switzerland, Italy, and Spain. The band then high-tailed it to Japan, where they clocked in another eight gigs before heading Down Under to visit their Australian fans. Green Day caused a bit of trouble in the land of Oz during an April 1998 appearance on Australia's Recovery TV. They weren't scheduled to perform, but apparently felt like it and hijacked the house band's instruments for an impromptu performance of "The Grouch." Needless to say, the song's lyrics were not made for live TV, and the band was promptly escorted out of the studio, leaving Recovery TV to, um, recover.

Meanwhile, Green Day surprised everyone by pulling a trump out of their top hat: A tear-jerking string-laden ballad called, "Good Riddance (Time of Your Life)." The song shocked the hell out of us all, and reached the upper numbers in all sorts of singles charts including the Adult Top 40. Adult?!? The video is, well, moving, and a true departure for the band. It is simple, featuring an uncharacteristically tranquil Billie Joe strumming an acoustic guitar at home while the camera lens flashes to a moment in the lives of people from all stations of life. The only sedate video the band had ever made won them the first MTV Video Music Award after thirteen prior nominations. The song touched a chord. "Good Riddance" ushered England out of the 1998 World Cup and the beloved cast of *Seinfeld* out of the show's final episode. It was polled as one of the top ten songs the British would like played at their own funerals. Interestingly, the song was actually written around the time of *Dookie* in ode of the infamous ex-girlfriend who left Billie Joe for Ecuador. It took Green Day's newly experimental bent while recording *Nimrod* to convince the band to take the chance in releasing the song, and the bet certainly paid off. The song was to be a concert-closer for years to come.

Accident-prone Mike (remember Woodstock?) continued to exhibit his amazing capacity for injury. April's booboo of the month—this time self-inflicted—took place during the band's April 17, 1998 performance for MTV's *Live From the Ten Spot* at San Francisco's Bottom of the Hill club. An overzealous stage jump resulted in his bass and his face colliding, and he had to leave the stage for a couple of songs before his bloody return. He played the rest of the show with a constant nosebleed. Much more serious was an incident at L.A. radio station KROQ's annual Weenie Roast on June 20th at the Irvine Meadows Amphitheater. The charity gig, always a lot of fun for the crowd and bands alike featured a stellar lineup this time around with performances by Creed, Deftones, Everclear, Madness, Marcy Playground, Third Eye Blind, and many more. Green Day's set was well underway when Third Eye Blind bassist Arion Salazar appeared onstage and surprised Mike with a bear-hug from behind. An altercation ensued and the confrontation continued backstage after the set. Mike was struck in the

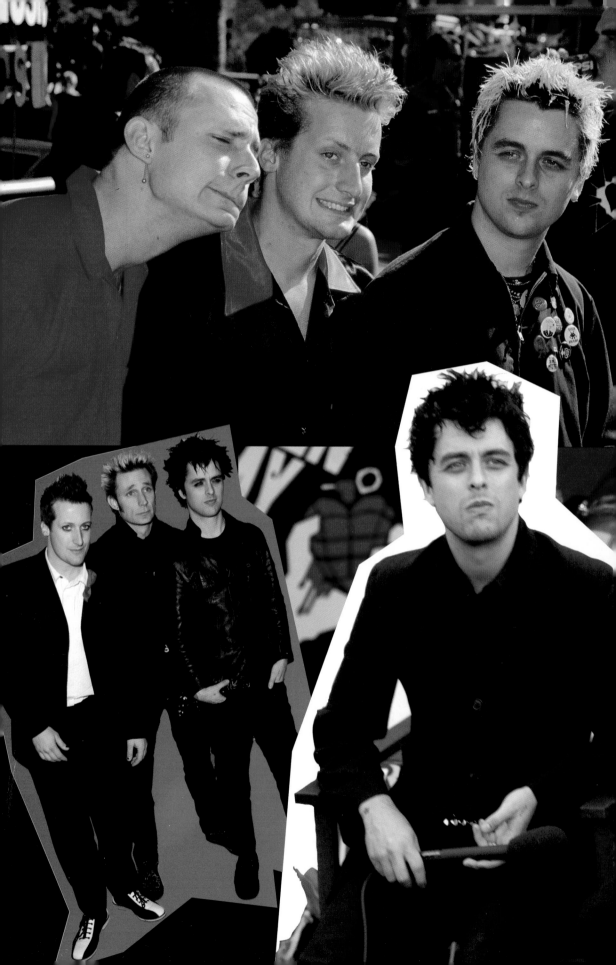

head with a beer bottle and was hospitalized with a fractured skull. Initial reports put the beer bottle in Salazar's hand, but Third Eye Blind quickly insisted it was an unidentified intervening fan who had struck Mike. Salazar issued a written statement saying, "I am sorry that my attempt at doing something I thought would be funny escalated into Mike getting hurt. That was never my intention. I simply had too much to drink and made a very bad decision. If I had been in Mike's place, I would have acted similarly. My heart goes out to him and I hope he recovers quickly. We have many friends in common and I just hope that he can accept my sincerest apology. I am sorry Mike." Green Day kept mum on the subject, and it was subsequently reported that the band had hired a private investigator to look further into the matter. The two bands would put the whole thing behind them within a year after a chance encounter between Mike and Three Eye Blind guitarist Kevin Cadogan at, naturally, a florist. Cadogan was purchasing a card to accompany a guitar as a get-well gift for a Berkeley kid who had been stabbed in the face. "Mike was really moved by this whole thing," Third Eye Blind frontman Stephan Jenkins told MTV on May 20, 1999. "It was really sort of this example of much greater strife ending much smaller strife. So it was a good thing."

The third leg of the *Nimrod* tour rolled on, having started on April 30th in Houston, Texas. While in New York City the band stopped off to pay a visit to pals David Letterman and Howard Stern. In Washington, D.C. they played the beloved annual WHFStival at RFK Stadium. Headlining alongside Green Day were Everclear, Foo Fighters, and Scott Weiland; Bad Religion, Marcy Playground, the B-52s, and the Mighty Mighty Bosstones also joined in the fun. Green Day had invited No Doubt trumpet

player Stephen Bradley and trombonist Gabe McNair to join them on tour commencing with their May 9th Asbury Park, New Jersey show as replacement for Voodoo Glow Skulls' Joe McNally and Brodie Johnson. "You use it in moderation," Mike said of the adopted horn section in a May 22, 1998 interview with the *Minneapolis Star Tribune*. "They're really cutting loose. It's like our tour bus drove through a circus and a lot of the circus creatures hung onto our bus. When we show up to town, it's like Ringling Bros. and Green Day's Circus."

Nimrod's third single, "Redundant," was pure pop. Billie Joe toned down his signature snarl as he sang the chorus *"Now I cannot speak / I lost my voice / I'm speechless and redundant / 'Cause I love you's not enough / I'm lost for words."* Green Day were continuing to showcase their musical growth on this album with this little gem.

Green Day turned down an offer to headline the 1998 Lollapalooza tour (as did Foo Fighters, Garbage, and Marilyn Manson) and the grandfather multi-act tour that had spawned so many others pulled its own plug, opting out of the concert circuit that year. Billie Joe, Mike, and Tré preferred to carry on with their own virtually nonstop tour schedule that washed its hands of North America on August 1st at the twelve-hour musical extravaganza called End Fest in Seattle. The grand finale of summer radio station-sponsored festivals (this one courtesy of KNDD) offered up some twenty acts and featured an air-conditioned electronica pavilion. It was Green Day's blistering hour-long set that would not soon be forgotten, however. Billie Joe took the stage in a manic mood and verbally assaulted the crowd with a stream of expletives. A barrage of red-hot tunes was to follow, punctuated by the frontman donning a red devil mask, mooning the fans, and bringing one of the moshers up on stage to take over guitar duties. The band said a memorable thank you and good night by setting fire to Tré's drum kit.

It was back to Europe for the rash of summer festivals in August. Green Day called it a day after the August 30th Pukkelpop Festival in Belgium, and took a well-deserved break after eight straight months of touring. As it turned out, the break was timed to coincide with a very exciting and completely non-band-related event, as Billie Joe was due to become a father for the second time. In September 1998, Adrienne Armstrong gave birth to a second son named Jakob Danger.

The band couldn't resist squeezing in a few more shows to round out the year and headed south to play seven shows in Argentina, Chile, and Brazil in November before calling it a day. They also offered up one last single with a hilarious video. The NFL-themed clip for "Nice Guys Finish Last" debuted on MTV's Total Request Live in December. It was filmed at Santa Clara, California's College of the Canyons in November, but nearly didn't happen as L.A. radio station KROQ leaked the news of the shoot and college officials balked at the likelihood of their campus being overrun by Green Day fans. KROQ announced the cancellation of the local video shoot after the college pulled the permit, and the reassured officials acquiesced and the show went on. Directed by Evan Bernard, the football take works beautifully, complete with cheerleaders, a crowd-surfing mascot, and an injury (Mike, of course).

Billie Joe, Mike, and Tré partied up in style to ring in the New Year by performing live from MTV's Times Square studios in New York City along with fellow acts Aaliyah, Limp Bizkit, and Method Man. The event, hosted by Jennifer Love Hewitt and Carson Daly, competed for viewers with Dick Clark's New Year's Eve special.

The New Year started off with a wee bit of controversy. Just days after the official announcement that Green Day would fill the support slot on five February dates of the *Rolling Stone's* No Security tour, the band pulled out. Other support acts including Bryan Adams, Jonny Lang, the Goo Goo Dolls, and the Coors offered to fill the Green Day-vacated spots. Despite speculation, the reason for the band's change of mind was never quite clear. It seems the band needed a break.

WAKE UP

The break turned out to be a year-and-a-half-long sabbatical during which the three men consciously decided to bow out of the limelight, reconnect with their families, and take their time musically instead of rushing to record another album.

"I think we were pretty burned coming off tour," Billie Joe told *USA Today* in its October 6, 2000 edition. "I spent so much time away from my kids. My wife was having a baby. I was sort of a wreck, and I really needed to get back in the swing of my family life and my kids and my personal life. You have to have your own life, and you have to explore things on your own to be able to write good songs that people can relate to. I just don't want to be one of those guys singing about the next hotel room."

It used to be occasion to break out the champagne when an album went Gold (selling 500,000 copies in the U.S.). Nowadays, Gold is a bit of a yawner—it's Platinum certification (one million copies), and subsequent multi-Platinum numbers—that is something to brag about. Well, in March of 2000 the Recording Industry Association of America inaugurated an all-new level to aspire to in the Diamond Award, a certification for album sales of over ten million. Of the sixty-two all-time best-selling albums that were certified Diamond, *Dookie,* with ten million sales, was duly honored. Top of the list, tied with twenty-five million copies sold, were Michael Jackson's *Thriller* and The Eagles *Greatest Hits.* If someone had pulled the Green Day three aside in the early '90s at a Gilman Street gig and told them that in the New Millennium one of their punk band's future albums would achieve sales in the league of The Beatles, Pink Floyd, Billy Joel, Led Zeppelin, AC/DC, Madonna, Metallica, Elton John, and Eric Clapton, no doubt the notion would have been greeted with a sneer worthy of Johnny Rotten.

The band reappeared on the scene very briefly for a live appearance at the 13th Annual Bridge School Benefit weekend-long concert to raise funds for the school for severely disabled children. The sold-out Mountain View, California November 1999 concerts enjoyed audiences of some 20,000 each night. Neil Young-driven benefits had been held since the school opened in 1987, and this year on the bill was headlining act The Who, Pearl Jam, Smashing Pumpkins, Beach Boys mastermind Brian Wilson, Tom Waits, Sheryl Crow, Lucinda Williams, and Emmylou Harris. Green Day played a string of hits, as well as debuting a new song called "Warning."

Billie Joe gave fans jonesing for a little Green Day a bit of a Christmas gift in the form of an announcement that the band would soon be back in the studio to record a new album. However, they wouldn't be working with Rob Cavallo. Rather they had decided upon a new producer by the name of Scott Litt. Litt was an accomplished record smith with a résumé including work with the Replacements, Patti Smith, Nirvana, Liz Phair, and no less than six R.E.M. albums. "I'm excited about [the album.] Some of the songs I've heard are really special," he told *Rolling Stone* on January 12, 2000. More good news was soon to follow when it was reported that Green Day was to join the Warped Tour that summer. But not so fast: By mid-February word was out that the Green Day-Scott Litt partnership was off. Neither party commented on the parting of ways.

Mike celebrated the New Millennium by releasing an album courtesy of his side project, The Frustrators. The album's title? *Bored in the U.S.A.,* a piss-take on the Bruce Springsteen classic. Record label? None other than Billie Joe and Adrienne Armstrong's own Adeline Records. The couple had started up the label with business partners and friends Jim and Lynn Thiebaud in late 1997. The Frustrators track, "Great Australian Midget Toss," was played during the NBA finals in L.A. on June 19, 2000. The Little People of America issued a statement in protest saying, "This sends out the wrong message to short-statured individuals and their families. The fact that it was used as a taunt at a major sporting event only makes it worse." The song features the lyrics, "*Hate to land them on their face / Those little guys are hard to replace.*" Mike's response on The Frustrators website was, "We have no problem with people of short stature or any other stature. For the record, I would like to state firmly that The Frustrators think violence is stupid and that we have a sense of humor about ourselves and the world.

If anyone has taken offense at our jokes, we do apologize for the misunderstanding."

Green Day set out to record in Oakland's 880 Studios at the beginning of April 2000 with Rob Cavallo back as a part of the process after the Litt split. After all, their lengthy hiatus wasn't spent island-hopping in the Caribbean; the three men had been dividing their time daily between their families and that all-enduring band practice. As Mike told MTV on August 7, 2001, "We have a super-serious work ethic. I don't know any band our size who practices as much as we do. But playing together is just what we know, and when we're not doing it for a couple days we start feeling lazy and bored." By the time it was time to record, the band hit the ground running. They knew the entire album inside and out. "We're not really sprinting. We're working at the same pace, but it's a pretty fast pace for recording," Tré told MTV on May 20, 2005. "We're faster than every other band, pretty much. That's what I've been told."

880 Studios, housed underneath a highway, provided the added dimension of console-rumbling traffic. The band brought quite a few unusual elements to the mix. Tré's concept of hiring two dominatrix to add some authentic sound effects to the recording of the track "Blood, Sex, and Booze" was truly inspired. In a July 26, 2000 interview with BBC Radio One's Steve Lamacq, Billie Joe revealed the rather unorthodox "Blood Sex Booze" sample, saying, "That's our engineer Tone taking his first flogging. Tone's our nineteen-year-old engineer. We brought in a very professional dominatrix, Mistress Simone, and she just cracked at him. I think it was his first experience of pain. . .we set mikes up in the room and recorded the whole thing and that's the intro to the song." Other guests included a mariachi band, a saxophonist, and Benmont Tench, keyboardist for none other than Tom Petty and the Heartbreakers.

Here is a band that truly loves the creative process. Tré raved about atmosphere in the studio to MTV during a June 1, 2000 interview, saying, "F***in' heavy emotions, man. It's really happy, really tense sometimes. When we're here and we're partying, we're partying good, we're partying hard. When we're working, we're working hard. Ideas have just been flowing around this place, like, just f***ing bouncing everywhere. We've kind of lost our minds a little bit, actually. . .in a good way. It's, like, a blessing to lose our minds in such a way. We're in creative mode for such a long time now. It's like we can't stop." Literally. Billie Joe woke his wife up in the middle of the night singing one of the new songs—in his sleep.

A WARPED WARNING

Time to get warped! Green Day set out on the sixth annual Warped Tour with the new album in the bag but not to be released until September. The traveling circus of music, sports, and all things punk gave its young audience a day (and night) to remember. This was an eight-hour show utilizing five stages to showcase over forty bands including Papa Roach, NOFX, Chuck D, the Long Beach Dub Allstars, and Mighty Mighty Bosstones. Extreme sports exhibitions such as skateboarding, BMX, and motocross filled in the bill. For just $25, concertgoers got real bang for the buck with more music and action than they could swallow. Ten semis schlepped the stages, sound, and light equipment. Four hundred-fifty bodies traveled on the tour including the artists, crew, and sponsors. "It is an expensive show to keep on the road, and we would not be able to do it without the sponsors," Kevin Lyman, the tour organizer, told *Amusement Business* in its May 8, 2000 issue.

"We've got to stake our claim a little bit, to remind everybody who's the best," Tré Cool candidly told MTV in a June 1, 2000 interview. "We haven't played live for a while, and I think people are forgetting. There's a lot of imitators out there, so we've got to remind people. . .They remember, but if they can't get Pepsi, they're going to get RC, you know. They can't get the real, they're going to get the substitute."

"We're amped about going on it," Billie Joe told *Rolling Stone* in its March 28, 2000 issue. "I'll get to skateboard every day, which will be fun—but you're not going to get me on the vert ramp." Even punks have to be sensible. Although really, what's a tour without a few war wounds? Tré took over for Mike in the accident-prone category during the tour and sustained a concussion and sacrificed part of one of his toes when his cymbals went flying.

Warping its way from the opening gig on June 24th in Phoenix, Arizona across the country to the East Coast, up to Canada, down to Florida, and winding down with five Texas stops, the tour was virtually non-stop, with an incredible 39 shows in just 44 days. No Doubt, Lit, and the Black Eyed Peas jumped onstage to join up with the traveling show on July 11th at the Minneapolis, Minnesota show. The July 15th stop off at New York City's Randalls Island was rained out and the tour gave up one of its very rare days off to reschedule for July 24th. Green Day missed the final Texas leg of Warped due to commitments for concerts in Japan. The band did not use its summer tour to test run any of the new material on their forthcoming album, however, choosing instead to remind their fans of their respectable back catalogue and whet their appetites for more.

Reprise Records offered up a funny promo for the new album that was entitled *Warning* on its website in the form of a mock presidential campaign. Candidate Billie Joe Armstrong's slogan? "Burning the Bridge to the 21st Century." Mike plays his running mate, and Tré his wife in the clip, which also features a faux ad from the opposition ("What do you really know about Billie Joe Armstrong? Did you know that he's a dick? And that he has a really ugly wife?").

As was becoming tradition, the band headed to Europe for a pre-album promotional tour. On September 15, 2000 the band played a "secret" gig for an invite-only crowd of 500 at Kings College London to preview tracks from *Warning*. It was a rousing success. "As tonight proves," the *NME* review testified, "the competition can't hold a torch to their infallible tunes and shabby charisma. Stoopid to the point of genius." The band was up to its old tricks again at a September 17th late-night in-store

appearance in London at the Virgin Megastore on Oxford Street on the eve of the release of the album's first single "Minority." They trashed their gear and spray-painted "Green Day" and "Goodnight" on the walls before the clock chimed midnight and fans were free to purchase the single.

Just two days before the album dropped, Green Day played yet another charity concert, the Big Day Out benefit in Atlanta, Georgia. Joining Stone Temple Pilots, Deftones, Everclear, Travis, Eve, Incubus, Linkin Park, and Papa Roach, they helped raise money for the nonprofit organization called Angel Flight which provides free air transportation for medical purposes for patients who cannot afford it.

Fall of 2000 saw the infectious "Minority" topping the *Billboard* Modern Rock Tracks, keeping company with a varied host of other *Billboard* current faves like Christina Aguilera, Ricky Martin with his hit "She Bangs," Limp Bizkit, Destiny's Child, and Shaggy. The single's video was directed by Evan Bernard whose past work had included videos for the likes of the Beastie Boys, as well as Green Day's own "Nice Guys Finish Last." The band shut down two downtown blocks in San Diego for the filming of the punk version of the Macy's Thanksgiving Day Parade. The multicolored Green Day float, complete with enormous balloon versions of the guys, is led down the empty streets by a squad of punk girl baton-twirlers. The fact that there is no audience is in keeping with the song's theme of rejoicing in one's outsider status *(I want to be the minority / I don't need your authority / Down with the moral majority / 'Cause I want to be the minority)*. The parade and the party's all over when the band trash their float and cut the balloons free.

Warning debuted at Number Four on the *Billboard* charts with 155,000 copies sold, in the venerable

company of Radiohead's Number One debuting *Kid A,* which sold 207,000 units. The two albums also came in at the same Number Four and Number One positions on the U.K. charts. Adeline Records stepped in to issue the requisite vinyl LP.

Reviews were by and large very favorable, with the odd thumbs-down. "Punk bands don't tend to age gracefully, but on its latest release Green Day proves that, after almost ten years of making music, three-chord power rockers can, in fact, grow up," *Billboard* observed in its October 14, 2000 issue. A day after the album dropped *Rolling Stone* proclaimed, "*Warning* finds Green Day growing out of adolescent snot-core and into the lost Beatles album they always had in them." The U.K.'s *NME* was less enthralled, observing, "If you ever needed proof that the band had a tough time making *Warning,* then just take a listen to it. . .*Warning* is the sound of a band losing its way." MTV dubbed the album "a pure pop record." The U.K. music mag *Revolver* classed it "a much broader work than previous Green Day albums—a little less punk, a little more acoustic. But the main emphasis, as always, is on Armstrong's hooky, melodic songwriting." *Launch* declared it "potentially the band's most enduring album."

In reply to recognition of the more serious nature of *Warning,* Billie Joe told *Rolling Stone* on October 4, 2000, "I feel everything we've done has been serious. I think our antics sort of get in the way of what people think. But I think this one, for me personally, was a lot more articulate than the last one. The last couple of records I feel were sort of reacting to a time period, but this time I think we're making an action, and I think we're making bolder statements than we ever have before."

Green Day were also the first to admit to a bit of a sunnier attitude this time around. Billie Joe was quoted in *Rolling Stone* on January 12, 2000, as saying, "We're really excited about the new songs. The overtone in the lyrics seems to be more positive. Not in a Prozac sort of way, but more in the sense of surviving and living to tell about it and taking on new challenges." Tré previewed the slightly more sanguine nature of the lyrics this time around to MTV News on May 30, 2000, disclosing, "They're not all downers. I suppose people have described other songs we have as being happy music, and then once you get into the lyrics, it's like, 'Oh f***, that's kind of dark.' I don't think there's as much of that going on. You've still got some of that. It's got the sarcasm, it's got the snottiness, but it's got a little light at the end of the tunnel." Billie Joe was quick to qualify that his trademark rage was still in place; he was just progressing with regard to how he dealt with it. "I'm so filled with anger," he told *Rolling Stone* during an October 4, 2000 interview. "But I think the anger is just more channeled into things— you try to create something positive. I mean, if you don't, then you do turn into an angrier older man, and I don't want to be an angry older man, because to me it sounds like a bitter old fart."

Despite the album's success and the open-armed welcome back the band received during the Warped tour, there was a bit of hesitation to dive headlong into the extensive touring for which Green Day was known. In an interview with *Rolling Stone* the day after *Warning's* release, Billie Joe said, "We really don't know what our touring is going to be like. I mean, I have so much at home. [My wife] Adrienne and me were sitting here talking and we were like, "We're *adults.*" I have to be home. I have a two-year-old and a five-year-old, and when I leave, things fall apart. It's just too much for one person to handle. But I don't hate touring though—I love touring."

In direct contradiction to their multi-Platinum status, they stuck to their punk roots. With their brand new Top Ten album not out a week, Green Day set off on a mini-tour of free radio-station-sponsored gigs in small venues. They played Roseland Ballroom in New York City as well as Indianapolis, Atlanta, Boston, L.A., and Seattle in small clubs, and rather than showcasing their new material, they left it up to the audience to determine the set list by request. Moreover, the band played a slew of covers including Lynyrd Skynyrd's "Sweet Home Alabama," Cheap Trick's "Surrender," The Who's "My Generation," Billy Idol's "Dancing With Myself," and even an inspired bit of Michael Jackson's "Beat It." The now-traditional Green Day move of inviting fans onstage to perform continued, and Billie Joe and Tré traded places on guitar and drums. They might have been one of the biggest bands around, but they proved that their D.I.Y. ethic remained alive and well.

Green Day had played a host of covers live over the years, but on November 5, 2000, their live version of Joni Mitchell's "Big Yellow Taxi" was especially appropriate. Billie Joe sang the lyrics *"Don't it always seem to go / That you don't know what you've got 'til its gone? / They paved paradise and put up a parking lot"* on a stage erected across the Street from City Hall during Take Back San Francisco, an event protesting the city's rising rents and lack of support for the arts. With dot-comers gobbling up any and all available real estate, musicians—and the lower rent they had been paying—were being unceremoniously kicked out as club after club and rehearsal space after rehearsal space was shut down. Evictions and ceiling high prices were becoming the norm, but the last straw was the August sale and subsequent closure of San Francisco's Downtown Rehearsal, a space utilized by some 500 bands. Frustrated and saddened by the change in atmosphere in their hometown, historically known as a haven for artists, the creative community organized the event. A veritable marching band of musicians toting their respective instruments began their "Million Band March" in the Mission District and made their way to City Hall.

"The Bay Area in general is losing its culture, especially in SF, where it's almost a cliché to say that the dot-com companies are moving in to take over now. There is no rent control in SF, and as of September, over 2,000 musicians were kicked out of their practice spaces because they're turning the downtown area into a place for condominiums. And a lot of artists are losing their live/work spaces. It's kind of scary, because here is a city that thrived on its cultural diversity, and now it's basically just turning into a place for the high-tech boom." Billie Joe lamented during a December 10, 2000 *Launch* interview.

Green Day took part in the event, tagged an "anti-gentrification celebration" and broadcasted live by Berkeley radio station KPFA-FM, along with fellow musicians Victoria Williams, Mark Eitzel, Creeper Lagoon, Felonious, the Blind Boys of Alabama, Lisa Flores, the Gun and Doll Show, Zen Guerrilla, and Metallica's Kirk Hammett. The Take Back San Francisco promoter Ian Brennan told MTV on November 2, 2000, that Green Day were "very committed to the community. They stayed here; they're supporters of the music scene." Green Day played to an enthusiastic crowd, and Billie Joe was greeted with cheers when he announced to the audience, "I'm sorry, I don't work behind a computer. I work behind a f***ing guitar!"

The Green Day tour machine continued its seemingly nonstop trek around the globe. At the end of October they could be found in Australia. In November and December they hit a few more global hot spots, performing for Portuguese, Spanish, German, British, and Irish fans. Then it was back to the good old U.S.A. for a few radio-station-sponsored charity dates, including a hometown gig in San Francisco on December 15th and KROQ's annual Los Angeles Almost Acoustic Christmas alongside No Doubt, Weezer, Moby, and Coldplay. After a break for Christmas, the band hit fifteen U.S. pit stops in arenas and amphitheatres with Kansas band, the Get Up Kids, as support commencing January 11th in Dallas, Texas and winding down on January 27th in Tulsa, Oklahoma.

"Warning," the second single from the album by the same name, was an instant hit both in the U.S. and abroad. John Paul Ballantine of U.K. radio station Cool FM told *Music & Media* on December 23,

2000, "It's a fabulous song. Green Day is good rock 'n' roll and we've always liked it and played it here. It's refreshing to get something that isn't dancey—real musicians playing real music." Imagine that!

Billie Joe explained the concept behind the song, "Warning" to *Rolling Stone* on August 24, 2000, saying, "it's just sort of how like there's always these warning labels—'don't cross these lines,' 'don't do this,' 'don't do that,'—and how it can become really suffocating. I hate being told what I can and can't do. Pretty soon we're not going to be doing anything and all of us are going to be ordering our groceries through the Internet." The video is a delightful concept piece, following a young protagonist through a day spent defying all the warnings, from waking up and promptly removing the label from his mattress to rubbing soap in his eyes, drinking sour milk, running through the halls with scissors, eating a massive meal immediately prior to going for a swim, and operating heavy machinery after ingesting a bottle of cough syrup.

This time the New Year brought the threat of a lawsuit. A virtually unknown U.K. band from Cambridge called the Other Garden claimed that a song of theirs aptly entitled "Never Got the Chance" which was written by their lead singer Colin Merry in 1992 was "reworked" by Green Day into their international hit single "Warning." But of course. Exactly how Green Day was meant to have gotten hold of the obscure song was a good question, but the Other Garden explained that the hugely successful band may have heard it while touring in the U.K. at some point since the song had been sent out to British radio stations on a promotional CD. The Other Garden requested that Warner Chappell freeze all royalty payments to Green Day pertaining to "Warning," and reportedly planned to sue the band for $100,000. The Other Garden's attorney, Alistair Nicholas, told *NME.com* on January 16, 2001, "They have yet to return any of our calls. At present they're not taking it terribly seriously, but fairly soon we will be appointing local counsel in L.A. who will be on the ground and better placed to deal with them." MTV quoted Colin Merry on January 12, 2001 as saying, "It looks like the little bloke is going to get shafted." Green Day vehemently denied the plagiarism allegation, and issued a statement saying, "If the claimants carry out their threats to sue Green Day, such a lawsuit will be defended vigorously."

Lawsuit schmawsuit. Green Day was about making music, and the band's creative energies seemed to know no bounds, as, despite their impressive proliferation and insane touring schedule, the three musicians managed to find it in themselves to branch out beyond Green Day. Most recently, Billie Joe teamed up with the Go-Go's—one of California's original '70s punk outfits who went on to become a top pop act in the '80s—to co-write the band's single "Unforgiven" on their first new studio album in seventeen years. He also played guitar and sang back-up vocals on the *God Bless the Go-Go's* single. "[Green Day were] influenced by us," Go-Go's guitarist Jane Wiedlin told MTV on February 12, 2001. "And we ended up getting re-influenced by them." However, Billie Joe's collaboration with the Go-Go's was neither the first nor last musical side-project for a Green Day member. Mike continued his Frustrators gig, teaming up with singer Jason Chandler, drummer Art Tedeschi, and guitarist Terry Linehan whenever he had the chance. A sophomore effort from the band was released in early 2002—proudly sporting yet another piss-take of a title this time with U2 as the punks: *Achtung Jackass*. Tré let off some creative steam outside Green Day by playing Latino jam sessions with musician buds and

penning his own wacky take on country songs. Billie Joe continued to experiment with longstanding occasional side-band Pinhead Gunpowder, formed back in the early '90s by a group of guys all committed to their own full-time bands but looking to keep up that garage band mentality whenever they could get together. Pinhead Gunpowder (comprised of Billie Joe on guitar/vocals, Crimpshine's Aaron Cometbus on drums, Jason White of Chino Horde on guitar, and Bill Schneider from Monsula on bass) released an impressive number of EPs, as well as five full-length albums on both Lookout! Records and Adeline Records. "I think it's really good for all of us to do things on the side," Mike told MTV on August 7, 2001, "because it allows us to grow as musicians. The way I've learned to play my whole life is just by playing with different people. There's no study to it. You just let your music go through your life and it all seems to work."

After a mere six weeks off the road, the band hopped on a jet and headed to Japan for nine shows, playing major cities Tokyo, Osaka, Sendi, and Fukuoka two nights running as demand for the Northern Californian punk outfit's live show was so high amongst Japanese fans. On the way back from Japan, Green Day planned to stop off in Hawaii where they would be joined with their families and spend a bit of quality beach time. The powers that be had other plans, however, as management reportedly decided to cancel Green Day's March 25th scheduled concert at the University of Hawaii—which also meant the nixing the vacation—so that a video for *Warning*'s third single, "Waiting," could be shot. It was worth it. The joyous, house-party-themed video is a celebration of all that Green Day has achieved, and at the end, you just want to cheer.

On Easter Sunday 2001, punk rock icon Joey Ramone died at the age of 49. "I can firmly say that rock 'n' roll will not be the same without Joey Ramone alive," Billie Joe told MTV on April 17, 2001. "The one thing no one will ever be able to [capture] was how cool he was. He was rock 'n' roll coolness. The glasses. The leather jacket. And he barely moved a finger. He just stood there. . .If you think about every person who has been inspired by the Ramones, directly and indirectly, you're talking about half of what you hear on the radio today." Mike weighed in, saying, "Thanks always comes a day late and a dollar short, but my respect has and will always be there for the band that showed me that simple songs and a simple life could make you happy."

Green Day decided at the last minute to played to over 60,000 music fans at the annual HFStival in Washington, D.C. on May 29th, and brought their blistering set to a dramatic close by a bit of pyromania. Also appearing at the festival this year was one of the copycat pop-punk outfits, Good Charlotte, who shot a video for their HFStival-inspired song, "Festival Song" live during their set.

Enough fooling around. In mid-June Green Day began a monster summer of touring that would take the band to major markets around the world and satisfy crowds clamoring for that inimitable Green Day high. The band brought down the house in one of their favorite cites, Minneapolis, Minnesota on June 17th and wouldn't stop to take a breath until the end of August, forty-four shows later. The band played sold-out shows all across America to thousands of fans each night in amphitheatres and arenas in major cities coast to coast, as well as a couple of Canadian stop-offs. They brought Australian punk/rockabilly/ska act the Living End along as support, exposing yet another aspiring up-and-coming band to a huge audience. Kick-ass performances on both *Leno* and *Letterman* gave fans who couldn't make the live run a taste of what they were missing. "If people really want to know what we're about, they've just gotta see us live," Mike told MTV in an October 1, 2000, feature. "Because that's a culmination of all of our songs and how silly and how serious and how happy and mean and we can be. We're a live band."

KNOWLEDGE

Billie Joe, Mike, and Tré upheld their reputation as one of—if not *the*—best live bands around, and fans new and old were not disappointed. Green Day had become masters of mixing together all of their now-traditional ingredients to create one hell of a show. Request hours, major audience participation, cover versions, sing-alongs, confetti cannons, fan sit-ins, crowd diving, and the biggest mosh pit you've ever seen—it was all there. The creation of an all-fans band handpicked from the audience by Billie Joe for an impromptu session of Operation Ivy's "Knowledge" was a consistent winner, and the locally inspired names of the impromptu groups (i.e. the St. Louis Losers) was all part of the fun. Billie Joe—ever a Tasmanian devil when performing—took the stage sporting a leopard-print thong and donned a crown whilst singing "King for a Day," his rousing tribute to the joys of cross-dressing. His solo encore performances of "The Time of Your Life (Good Riddance)" never failed to bring the crazed energy of the whipped-up sea of fans to an instant halt, while thousands collectively held their breath in agreement as that inimitable voice washed over them.

Leaving the U.S. to recover from the onslaught, Green Day headed to Europe for the summer's rock festival season. The first stop was historic Avenches, Switzerland for the Rock Oz Arena festival at the stupendous amphitheatre, which seats tens of thousands. The band then jumped over to Germany for the Highfield Festival in Erfurt, the Bizarre Festival in Cologne, the Columbiahalle in Berlin, and the Gross Freiheit in Hamburg. The wonderful joint venture of rock events is England's Reading and Leeds festivals, held on the same weekend and swapping lineups, thereby cleverly holding the same massive concert in two places at the same time. This year Green Day joined the likes of Marilyn Manson, Eminem, Travis, Ash, Queens of the Stone Age, Manic Street Preachers, and the Strokes, playing Reading on Friday, August 24th, and Leeds on Saturday, August 25th. Concert attendees paid £80 for the weekend or £35 daily, and definitely got their quid's worth. "It is great when you can see an ocean of people in front of you," Billie Joe raved to *Kerrang* in its September 2004 issue. "I remember

at Reading we played before Travis, and someone said, 'How are Travis going to follow that?' I like how they used the word 'that.' I like the fact that people describe our live show by asking the question, 'How is someone going to follow *that?*'" It was on to the Glasgow Green for Scotland's 8th annual T in the Park, this year hosting over fifty bands including Weezer, Coldplay, Nelly Furtado, and David Gray. Green Day wound up their high-powered summer by performing in London on BBC DJ Steve Lamacq's Evening Session and by nabbing *Kerrang* magazine's Classic Songwriters award.

The band then took another one of those well-deserved breaks from the road, but kept themselves busy with their next project, a "Best Of" CD humorously entitled *International Superhits!* The band returned to Oakland's good old Studio 880 in September to lay down two new tracks with producer Jerry Finn. "Maria" (first released as the B-side to the international "Minority" single release and now re-recorded) and "Poprocks & Coke," would open the 21-track CD. The remaining 19 tracks make up a string of hits from *Dookie* through to *Warning.* Let's keep in mind what an impressive accomplishment this was—all of the bandmembers were still in their twenties. Released in mid-November of 2001, *International Superhits!* peaked at Number Forty on the *Billboard* album charts. Reprise released a limited-edition run of 4,000 purple and pink vinyl LPs. A fantastic visual retrospective in the form of an accompanying DVD appropriately entitled *International Supervideos!* was the icing on the cake. An hour-long journey through time with fifteen music videos from breakthrough clip "Longview" to latest release "Waiting," the DVD was truly a must for any Green Day fan—or fan-to-be.

Artists often have mixed feelings about "Best Of" compilations, and Billie Joe was no exception. "I remember at the time we didn't want to put out the best of, *International Superhits!*" Billie Joe told U.K. hardcore magazine *The Big Cheese* in its October 2004 issue. "But the thing about that was that part of our career is over: Here's the retrospective and we don't have to look back and we can move forward."

"Seeing a decade of your songs laid out like that is an invitation to midlife crisis," he told *Time* magazine in its January 31, 2005 issue. "Suddenly we were asking, 'Why are we in this band? Do we want to keep doing this? And, you know, what might happen if we challenged ourselves?'"

He admitted to the positive aspect of it, however, while reflecting on putting the hits collection together and listening to some of the older tracks to *Rolling Stone* in a November 26, 2001 interview. "I think that we've stuck to what we believe in. I don't feel like we've whored ourselves. Everything that we've achieved has come naturally to us. And everything that has come to us, it wasn't about some huge marketing plans. I think people genuinely liked our songs. A lot of bands have to trade in their integrity to get what they want, and the gross thing about it is that they have no problems doing it at all. I think we've accomplished a true sense of independence." He also laughingly admitted that it "would be really cool to look back on it and to pat myself on the back for once in my f***ing life."

The band cropped up here and there at the start of 2002, playing a one-off gig at the January Winter X-Games in Aspen, Colorado, but the big splash was their performance at the induction of the Ramones into the Rock and Roll Hall of Fame. After Eddie Vedder's rather lengthy speech, Green Day hit the stage to remind everyone just what the Ramones were all about, delivering a blistering 1-2-3 punch of a tribute by playing "Rockaway Beach," Teenage Lobotomy," and "Blitzkrieg Bop." They gained further props by promptly leaving the show directly after their performance without speaking to reporters, a move perceived as very punk-minded, although the band later claimed they had no idea that there was a press/photo session after the show. Regardless, they had made a memorable contribution to a momentous occasion.

Then disaster struck. After playing five concerts in Japan, Green Day embarked on a much-hyped co-headlining tour with one of the bands they had inspired (and who arguably would not exist had it not been for Green Day), Blink-182. Blink were the first to admit their debt to their co-headliners, telling *Rolling Stone* on April 16, 2002, "They were a huge influence for us. Green Day breaking punk rock into the mainstream consciousness really helped us and opened up people's minds to our kind of music."

The Pop Disaster tour set out on its forty-six-date trek on April 17, 2002 in Bakersfield, California. Jimmy Eat World was the main support for the first half of the tour, with Saves the Day taking their place for the second half. Green Day and Blink handpicked a slew of low-profile local bands to fill in the support-support slots throughout the tour. The tour was booked at mainly outdoor venues, with indoor alternatives utilized in states with late sunsets in order to maximize the full impact of the bands' significant light shows. Massive amphitheatres and arenas were packed to the gills, and in order to satisfy New York City fans, the bands were booked at both Madison Square Garden and Jones Beach. Each band played a 75-minute set, with Green Day playing first and Blink closing the show.

"There are a lot of issues here with both bands," Creative Artists Agency's Darryl Eaton told *Billboard* on March 2, 2002. "They are both very particular about production and where and when they play. There is a ton of attention to detail here." Expectations were high. "The bottom line is [that] this is going to be a great show," I.M.P. president Seth Hurwitz said. "These are two very, very entertaining bands, and people know this is a once-in-a-lifetime show. It's a real bargain, and these bands haven't forgotten that it's called 'show business.'" Blink-182's bass player Mark Hoppus promised *Rolling Stone* in its April 16, 2002 edition, "a bunch of fire and cool lights to distract people from our poor musical performance." "We're going to be bringing out our big production," Billie Joe said. "We're going to be biting the heads off bats."

The tour thundered on across the country, a veritable parade of rigs and buses. Green Day had their families on board, and playing around with the kids backstage and after the shows was a hell of a way

to unwind. Green Day's homecoming gig at the Oakland Arena on April 29th was a raging success, and the band donated all of the concert's proceeds to the Oakland Area Children's Hospital. It all came to a screeching halt on June 17th in Minneapolis.

Green Day had a few party tricks up its sleeve, including a beer-swilling pink bunny rabbit to introduce the band, an extra guitarist, Jason White (also a member of Pinhead Gunpowder and the Influents), ten-foot high columns of flames, and a horn section alternately dressed in mariachi garb and bee and chicken outfits. The now-legendary on-stage creation of a new band made up of lucky audience members was a staple of the Green Day set, but it was the pure Green Day energy and killer tunes that ensured that Blink-182 had a very hard act to follow. The inevitable comparisons between the two bands had reviewers and fans casting their vote for Green Day. "What Green Day's successors (Blink-182 and their ilk) fail to recognize is that the cartoon isn't enough, that there has to be driving force behind it," *Variety* observed in its July 30, 2001 issue. *Billboard's* review of the April 26th Los Angeles show noted, "The concert cast Green Day in the role of punk elders, showing up Blink-182 with a confidence and efficiency that the latter has not yet mastered," and added, "when you let a second-rate Green Day perform after the real Green Day, the end result is a nearly three-hour show that stumbles to a close." Ouch. Could it be that Green Day's subconscious motivation on this tour was to upstage the younger punk upstarts? Show 'em who's boss? Who knows, but Billie Joe's stage entrance—jumping on top of a monitor to demand of the crowd "Who's your f***ing daddy?!?"—said something, that's for damn sure.

RARITIES

What better title for an album-full of rarities and B-sides from the infamous punk pranksters than *Shenanigans?* Green Day released the fourteen-song compilation in July 2002, and the CD peaked at Number Twenty-Seven, considerably and rather surprisingly higher than *International Superhits!* Reprise also released a blue vinyl LP. *Rolling Stone* gave the album a miserly two stars although noting, "In retrospect, this collection of odds and sods ... proves Green Day were every bit as passionate as their first-generation punk heroes." *NME,* on the other hand, was quite taken by the assortment of non-hits, and opined that the new song on the album, "Ha Ha You're Dead," with lyrics courtesy of Mike rather than Billie Joe, "Proves Green Day, broadly, still have it: A chugging playground nose-thumbing that finds these three fathers stubbornly refusing to grow up." *Shenanigans* also offered up two covers, one of the Ramone's "Outsider" and a punked-up version of the Kinks' "Tired of Waiting for You." All in all, the outcome of Green Day having effectively cleaned out their closet was a success.

Green Day gave themselves three weeks to catch their breath after the Pop Disaster run and then went on a eight-date blitz in the U.K. to remind British fans who *their* daddy was. They headlined the second night of the Virgin Move festival on July 11th held in Manchester at the Old Trafford Cricket Ground. As national U.K. newspaper *The Guardian* amusingly observed in its July 13, 2002 review of the concert, "Twenty-five years ago, the idea of a punk group playing the hallowed turf of a major cricketing establishment would have resulted in questions in the House." (House of Parliament to you.) As a matter of fact, the thousands of female punksters in the crowd were scoring quite a victory unbeknownst to them, as only a few years ago women were banned from the cricket ground's bar. Green Day took a day off and then played the Witness Festival in Dublin, Ireland before returning to Scotland's T in the Park on July 14th. The Newcastle Arena was next on the headlining tour de force, followed by an incredible two sold-out nights at the one and only Wembley Arena in London. Green

Day then scared the hell out of Cardiff Castle's famous peacocks, playing a July 19th concert on the Welsh castle's grounds with none other than Iggy Pop as support. They wrapped the United Kingdom up with a final show at Nottingham's Wollaton Park on July 20th. Tens of thousands of U.K. fans had been duly done and dusted, Green Day style.

In November 2002, Billie Joe posted an audio message on the band's official website encouraging fans to visit *greenday.net* in order to sign an online petition against the war in Iraq, saying, "For those of you who are opposed to the war in Iraq, I want to start a petition on *greenday.net* to send to George W. Bush strongly urging him to rethink his plans for military invasion. This petition isn't only for people who live in America, but people all over the world."

All was quiet on the Green Day front until the headline-grabbing news that Billie Joe had been arrested for drunk driving. On January 5, 2003 at 1:00 AM he was pulled over in Berkeley near Telegraph Avenue for speeding in his black BMW convertible, was Breathalyzed, and failed the requisite sobriety test. He was taken to jail for the remainder of the night, booked, and released the next morning on $1,200 bail. Berkeley Police reported that he was "very cooperative" and that he did not mention that he was famous.

Months went by with nary a peep. In June 2003, Tré jokingly offered up a bone chip from a recent knee operation to fans on the band's official website. After receiving serious inquiries he responded with an audio message addressing "You little freaky weirdoes" announcing a haiku contest to win the bit of bone. "I alone will judge," he said. "Good luck bastards."

Billie Joe joined a cast of punk and hardcore artists to contribute to the John Roecker stop-motion animated movie *Live Freaky! Die Freaky!* produced by Rancid's Tim Armstrong for his Hellcat Pictures. Billed as "an Epic motion picture of puppet proportions," the film is set in the year 3069 when Charles Manson emerges in the midst of a wasteland to lead a group of straggling Apocalypse survivors. Billie Joe is the voice of Manson. "I don't know where that voice came from," Billie Joe told *Rolling Stone* on February 25, 2004. "It was like I was possessed by the character." The film also features the entire cast and crew of Rancid in Lars Frederiksen, Matt Freeman, Brett Reed, and Tim Armstrong; Good Charlotte twins Benji and Joel Madden; Blink-182's Travis Barker; NOFX's Fat Mike; and quite a few more. Roecker's ties with the West Coast punk community began in the Seventies. He and X singer Exene Cervenka co-owned the L.A. shop You've Got Bad Taste. Roecker also organized the 1999 Punk Hall of Fame Awards.

Anyone wondering where the hell Green Day had disappeared to had only to look as far as the band's home away from home, Oakland's own Studio 880. The studio, which had broken ground in 1998 had since expanded from one room to a complex featuring three recording studios, film/video post-production suites, and professional offices. Billie Joe and Mike were on hand for the December 11th Studio 880 holiday party, and Mike cut the ribbon on the opening of the brand new Studio C. Aside from Green Day favoring the studio, it has also been utilized by the likes of Iggy Pop, Smash Mouth, Chris Isaak, Third Eye Blind, and, rather coincidentally, a band called the Network. In addition to its world-class equipment, 880 offers other amenities such as a full kitchen, bars, a basketball court, and slot car racing. In fact, in addition to working on their own new material the band spent some time in the studio with Iggy Pop, contributing to a few tracks on Iggy's upcoming 2003 album *Skull Ring. Skull Ring* was released to critical acclaim and featured two tracks co-penned by Billie Joe and Iggy, "Private Hell" and "Supermarket." *Billboard's* November 22, 2003 review of the album noted, "Hearing Pop sing with Green Day on the slick 'Supermarket' feels somewhat like a revelation."

All was well in the punk rock world. Green Day had wrapped up an albums-worth of material provisionally entitled *Cigarettes and Valentines* at 880 and were just about to ready it for release. Then, one day in November 2002, the band turned up at the studio to discover that the master tapes of their fully completed new album were gone. Stolen. Lifted. Gone. Why and where they are today is still a mystery. No one ever demanded money in exchange for the masters' safe return, and none of the tracks has ever turned up on the Internet or on a bootleg. Just gone.

OF RAGE AND LOVE

Billie Joe, Mike, and Tré were incredulous. They sat down with Rob Cavallo who bluntly asked them whether they had really given their all to create the lost material. The answer was no. Nor did they have it in them to try to lay it all down again. So, what to do? As it turned out, without the fateful theft, what was to be the trio's masterpiece, the punk rock opera *American Idiot*, would never have been made. Perhaps some punk deity stretched his tattooed arm down from the heavens above and plucked the masters from planet earth, deeming them Just Not Good Enough. "The gloves were off and we were just like, 'Let's just go for it, let's push ourselves to be maximum Green Day.' With the stuff that ended up getting stolen, looking back, I don't really think we were being maximum Green Day," Billie Joe told MTV on September 7, 2004.

After some fifteen years together, the bandmembers wisely sat down and took a good hard look at their three-way relationship and engaged in some much-needed open-heart surgery. They decided it was not for them to follow the all-too-common path of many a band whose members become bitter and hateful towards one another before inevitably ruining what was once a great creative collaboration. Green Day decided it was time to address the problems head-on. Billie Joe realized that although the three men interacted as adults with the outside world, when they were together they regressed to teen-aged level communication. He suggested that band practice, this time around, should include weekly talk sessions.

"We were being dicks to each other," Mike succinctly put it to *Kerrang* in its July 2004 issue. "We'd gotten kind of good at that. We wouldn't let each other speak and we certainly wouldn't listen to what each other was saying, and that led to some communication problems. We didn't go into therapy or anything like that, but it was something that we needed to deal with. Those kind of things can lead to real problems for a band; rifts develop and then suddenly you've got a group of people who aren't happy in each other's company any longer. And we were damn sure that that wasn't going to happen to us."

"There was a lot of talking going on with this record," Billie Joe told *Alternative Press* in its October 2004 issue. "And a lot of the growing-up process for us was like, 'Dude, you've been saying the same thing to me since you were fifteen, and I've been *hating* it for fifteen years!' We just let it all out and declared our places, and then felt comfortable in our places. And it was a very big deal, because now the weird thing is, we feel younger and more revitalized, and we're having more fun than we ever had." Billie Joe finally staked his claim as the band's songwriter. "We all had to look at each other and our roles and go, 'Who are you in this band? And it has nothing to do with who you were when you were sixteen in this band.' We're all over thirty now. Who are we now?" he told *Entertainment Weekly* in November 2004. "For the first time, I got recognized as the songwriter. Just in the last two years. That was sort of a battle. I'm the singer and the guitar player, and I write all the songs. So sometimes there was a little bit of envy that comes up."

"I think we just looked outside of ourselves as individuals, too, and kind of did a little bit of work on ourselves," Mike told MTV on September 21, 2004. "We sat and asked ourselves the hard questions that maybe most couples don't want to ask themselves." (Which prompted Tré to clarify, "We're more than a couple, we're a triple.") "We like each other a lot, which is a problem. Because not being afraid to fail in front of those closest to you is the most difficult thing in the world. We needed to get to where we could look stupid in front of each other—artistically speaking," Mike told *Time* magazine in its January 31, 2005 issue. "Fear of failure is the biggest impediment to success," he declared in a September 1, 2004 *Bass Player* interview. "There's no such thing as a stupid question or idea. You just need to be honest with yourself." It's perhaps not so surprising that these three men were able to sort out and reevaluate their relationships without outside help. After all, they had each been addressing life's issues on their own since they were just kids.

Billie Joe also took a month-long sabbatical of sorts, taking a solo trip to New York, which by all accounts involved a lot of barhopping. "He was really questioning what he was doing," his wife Adrienne told *Rolling Stone* in its February 24, 2005 issue. "It was scary, because where he had to go to get this record wasn't a place I'm sure I wanted him to be."

The lead singer wasn't the only one with internal emotional crises. "Right before going in to record this, I got married," Mike told *Revolver* in its March 2005 issue. "And the day we finished it, my wife said, 'I can't do this anymore.' We'd been together seven years, and she finally knew that she's always gonna play second fiddle [to the band]. She's still very supportive of this, but she had to be honest with herself." Tré also admitted to shedding more than a few tears during the making of the album; he was in the midst of his second divorce to wife Claudia with whom he had a young son, Frankito.

The bandmembers began hashing out songs, or, more precisely, pieces of songs. Anything and everything was game. They began "writing things outside of ourselves," as Tré put it in *Drum!* Magazine's December 2004/January 2005 issue. "New wave, Latin, polka, all different styles. . .It was like, 'If you're not doing anything, do something. It doesn't matter what it is. Don't think in terms like this has got to be the next Green Day single, or this has to be something for the album. If it's inside, get it out.' Throw it at the wall and see what sticks, you know?" It was fun; it was freeing.

Billie Joe told *AMP* magazine in its December 2004/January 2005 issue, "I would come up with an idea for a song and then an hour later I would convince myself it was terrible. And Rob [Cavallo] was great for sort of talking me off the ledge. . .Rob had an undaunted faith. He kept saying, 'Just go.'" They also opened their minds to a wide range of influences, from the Clash and David Bowie, The Who and Bob Dylan, to *Grease, West Side Story,* and the *Rocky Horror Picture Show*. As time went on the trio became more and more emboldened. "It was really, really nice for all of us just to really follow through on songs," Mike told *USA Today* on September 7, 2004. "A lot of the time a song will be abandoned on the guitar, [because] you're all, 'Ah, that's not going to be cool.' Well, maybe just follow through and see where you get, and at the end of it, if it still sucks, maybe you learned something."

One day Mike composed a little (literally—we're talking thirty seconds long) ditty when he was on his own in the studio (lyrics: *Everyone left the studio / Everyone left the studio / Everyone left the studio / But me)*. The silly, vaudeville mini-song delighted Billie Joe, who set out to write his own thirty-second bit. Tré took the hook and the trio began competing with one another to come up with more, and better, bits and pieces and the idea to tack them all together spawned the punk rock opera concept. Crazy. Not a real idea, just. . .But the notion and the atmosphere soon took on a vital edge. "It was funny at first," Billie Joe told *Entertainment Weekly* in its September 17, 2004. "But then something more serious started happening. We were like, 'It's fun, it's dramatic, we feel like we're living up to our ambitions and expectations as musicians, so let's just do it.' I think the biggest doubt was that people would think we're f***ing crazy."

Before they knew it, the band was in a creative groove that was too good to slow down; they began spending all day in the studio making music, and all night hanging out talking music. Their enthusiasm for music, music, and more music inspired them to set up a pirate radio station in "the warehouse," the band's rehearsal space behind Adeline Records' Berkeley H.Q. so that they could send music out over the local airwaves. The trio even laid down a CD's-worth of "inappropriate" Christmas songs. "A lot of things got wrapped into it," Mike told *Inside Connection* in its January 2005 issue. "Some of it turned out absolute crap; some of it turned out brilliant."

And some of it, it seems, turned up on Adeline Records. A mysterious new wave-inspired synth album entitled *Money Money 2020* by an unknown band called The Network surfaced on Adeline Records at the beginning of October 2003, and the lead singer had an infectiously familiar voice. Rumors that this was really a new Green Day album flew fast and wide, and although the band would never confirm or deny it, they made nudge-nudge-wink-wink references in the press. Mike told *Spin* in its November 2004 issue that while they were working on *American Idiot*, "We became so f***ing creative, we probably could've written a whole record in a day. It's arguable that certain records *were* written in a day. No Green Day records, of course." Of course. Further fueling speculation was the fact that The Network trio was made up of bandmembers whose faces aren't visible on the album artwork and who are called Captain Underpants, the Snoo, and Van Gogh. Using wacky pseudonyms isn't new to the Green guys. They've been checking into hotels under names like "Joe Lies" and "Rumple Stiltskin" for years now. Regardless, that they were in such a whirling dervish of a creative state that they would anonymously put out an entire album's-worth of material just to get it out of their collective system is quite amazing.

The joint reassessment of the band as three people and how they could better interact and of the band with regard to what kind of music they wanted to create led the trio down an explosively creative, ambitious path. Once "Jesus of Suburbia" was written, that path was clear, and the bar was set. As Tré told *Revolver* in its March 2005 issue, "After that song was written, we knew where we had to go. As scary as it was to be at the bottom of a mountain that high, we knew that we had to get to the top of it. We were not gonna settle for any regrets, any feeling that we could have done it better. It was like, here we go!"

"I kept getting blown away in the studio," Rob Cavallo told *Entertainment Weekly* in its February 11, 2005 issue. "Every time they'd turn something in, I'd be like, 'Holy s***, this is f***ing great!' I've been doing A&R a long time, and there are always signs that tell you if a record's going to work. I started to see every sign you could possibly see." His enthusiasm was shared by record company execs. Reprise's senior vice president of promotion told *Billboard* on October 9, 2004, "When I first spoke to Billie Joe about it at the beginning of the project, I was left with the impression that there was going to be little if anything for radio. Then, lo and behold, when I was invited to the studio, I was speechless, because I heard so many singles."

By the time the band left Oakland and hit Hollywood's Ocean Way Studios, they knew they had something special. In the absence of actual fireworks to mark the moment the band set to record the album's first track was an explosion; it was count down one, two, three—and BANG—a fire

started in one of the boxes. Billie Joe proved a dab hand with a fire extinguisher, and the band got on with business.

Billie Joe played the hell out of two of his favorite guitars on the album: A reissue 1959 Les Paul called Booty and a 1956 Les Paul Junior. "For this album we were like, 'Let's just go balls-out on the guitar sound—plug in the Les Pauls and Marshalls and let it rip," he told *Guitar World* in its Holiday 2004 issue. "I've never played as much guitar on a record as I did on this one. I decided that, when it's time for a solo, I'm gonna play the f***ing thing, whereas in the past I've held back, thinking, Nah, that might sound corny. But this record is sort of about being fifteen and rocking out in front of a mirror." And about putting aside all of those doubts and just, as they say, going for it.

The trio took a rather unconventional approach to the recording process for *American Idiot*. Rather than the usual route—drummer lays down all the drum tracks, up next is bass, then guitar, and finally all of the vocals are added—the band recorded each song one by one, in order. It just made sense.

Not playing it safe isn't easy. Putting your tried and tested career strategy out the window is daring. "For all we knew it was as likely to go to hell in a hand-basket as sell millions of records," Billie Joe told *Rock Sound* in its March 2005 issue. He put it bluntly to *Rolling Stone* on February 24, 2005, recalling, "We decided we were going to be the biggest, best band in the world or fall flat on our faces." Well, we all know what the outcome was. . .

But let's not get ahead of ourselves. The world's introduction to the punk-rock opera was via the release of the "American Idiot" single and video at the height of the summer, in August 2005.

Seemingly within seconds the song's opening verses, *"Don't want to be an American Idiot / Don't want a nation under the new mania / Can you hear the sound of hysteria? / The subliminal mind f*** America"* had burned into the consciousness of a disenfranchised and confused generation. *Billboard* immediately tagged the single in its "Picks—Singles Essentials" on August 28, 2004, and observed, "It has been four years since Green Day released a studio album, and judging from the immediate response to the title track from its forthcoming set, radio has indeed been waiting for its return," and added, "With the election ten weeks away, this song could not be more timely." Radio was as wildly enthusiastic about the single as it would normally be about the Next Big Thing rather than

about yet another song from a band whose first hit single hit the airwaves ten years prior. You can bet the suits at Reprise were happy. Senior vice president of promotion, Phil Costello, told *Spin* magazine in its November 1, 2004 issue, "I have nothing to compare it to. This never, ever happens."

Some radio stations took it upon themselves to bleep out the lyrics *"Maybe I am the faggot America / I'm not a part of a redneck agenda."* Whether they simply missed the point or were just afraid of the fine-happy F.C.C. is unclear. Billie Joe told U.S. gay and lesbian newsmagazine *The Advocate* on November 23, 2004, "There was a fear of people thinking I was using ['faggot'] in a derogatory way, but I thought of it as empowering. Hell, nobody ever called me 'redneck' in high school." The single peaked at Number One on the *Billboard* Modern Rock Tracks, Number Five on the Mainstream Rock Tracks, and Number sixty-one on the Hot 100.

As per recent custom, Green Day played a few major concerts before unveiling their new album— perhaps hitting the stage is their way of dealing with nerves—and August found them at the Summer Sonic festival in Japan, at the Ambassador in Dublin, Ireland, and kicking some serious ass at the U.K. 2004 Reading Festival. A strong list of contenders played the festival, but it was Green Day who brought down the house, playing a host of their own songs alongside covers of "Shout," "I Fought the Law," and a fitting "We Are the Champions." *Kerrang's* review of the gig tells it well, stating, "This is who the crowd have been waiting to see, this is why 50 Cent was dismissed so quickly, and the scrabble to get to the front is unholy. The Darkness may be the showmen, the White Stripes the darlings, but nobody does it better than Green Day. They're clearly up for it, too. This is the band at their best: Powerful, precise, and ripping through songs at the speed of light." Quite a review! Green Day closed the festival with a solo Billie Joe leading a sing-along of massive proportions to "Good Riddance (Time of Your Life)."

A very well timed September 20th appearance on *David Letterman* put the band on the show the same night as Democratic presidential candidate John Kerry, with whom the band enthusiastically posed for the photo op of the year. After all, who is the American Idiot? "It could be seen as being George Bush who's the idiot," Billie Joe told *Kerrang* in its July 2004 issue. "I suppose that might seem pretty obvious. But I think the title of the album works on more than one level. I know how Americans are often viewed by the rest of the world. We're seen as being dumb and arrogant, which is a pretty lousy combination. Americans talk about how our country is the best country in the world, which is something I don't notice people in a lot of other countries doing. And the people who say this loudest tend to be people who have often never been to another country. That's American idiocy for you."

Billie Joe explains the "redneck agenda" as "the Americanizing of places that don't want to be Americanized. Those people in Iraq are still part of a culture that's a lot older than ours and has nothing to do with the Western world. We can't think that we can just walk in and force these things upon people," he told *Revolver* in its March 2005 issue. "And the rednecks that are in office right now seem to feel that liberating people means taking their culture from them and sticking ours in—like, McDonalds and KFCs and Wal-Marts for everyone!"

"'*American Idiot*' is just about the confusion in what's going on today," he told MTV on August 10, 2004, "whether it's the non-reality of reality television or what you see on CNN. It's about what kind of fears are being imposed on me as a watcher of all this stuff, and just feeling completely confused and alienated."

Green Day made a very bold and very risky move, deciding to debut *American Idiot* live in its entirety—before and on the cusp of the album's release at intimate shows in L.A., Chicago, New York City, and Toronto. On September 16, 2004, the band took the stage at Hollywood's Henry Fonda Music Box Theatre and for the very first time commenced playing an album full of songs to a crowd that had only heard one of the tracks in their lives. And they loved every minute of it. If anything was to prove the strength of *American Idiot*'s material, it was for a live audience to react as enthusiastically to it on the first take as they would to a set of beloved familiar hits. "It seemed really scary to do," Mike told *Kerrang* in its 2004 Yearbook issue. "It's setting ourselves up for a fall, really, because when you're playing a nine-minute song to someone who's never heard it, you're basically playing to deer in the headlights. But we prevailed, thank goodness." As the strains of the piped-in pre-show music (the *Rocky Horror Picture Show* soundtrack), a pair of red and black attired burlesque hostesses ushered the band in by singing "*Nobody likes you / Everybody hates you*" before the curtain dropped and the drama commenced. The Green Day three augmented their power and did the material justice by adding an extra guitarist and two vocalists. The band rewarded the fans for their tremendous response to the brand new album by returning to the stage for a several-good-old-hits encore. As the *Hollywood Reporter* put it in its September 20, 2004 review of the concert, "Green Day have raised the stakes for themselves and their fans, taking things to another level, and leaving behind all punk-pop pretenders of the past few years. . .Debuting their new album, the once-hotshot punks become a great rock 'n' roll band, and it's glorious."

AMERICAN IDIOT

American Idiot debuted at no less than Number One, the very first time at the top slot on the *Billboard* charts for the band. Sales of 267,000 copies in the U.S. knocked R&B hot shot Nelly down to Number Two and had Green Day joining the company of a mixed bag in the Top Ten including Australian country singer Keith Urban, the legendary Ray Charles, and reality-TV-generated pop act Ashlee Simpson. And that's just in Green Day's homeland—*American Idiot* also debuted at Number One in Australia, Canada, Japan, and the U.K. with reported opening-week worldwide shipments of 1.5 million units. The album even topped cyber charts as iTunes music store's bestseller. "This is a band that believes in the communicative power of music and they have a point of view that keeps the public interested over a period of time," a happy Warner Brothers Records chairman/CEO told *Daily Variety* on September 30, 1994. "They are what we used to call a career band—great songwriting, great live act. They are reaching people all over the world."

But lots of albums have sold well. The difference here was that *American Idiot* garnered universal rave reviews the likes of which no band could fantasize. The word "masterpiece" was handed out like candy at Halloween. An across-the-board media love fest was underway a full decade after the three neopunks blasted their way onto the music world's consciousness. *Time* magazine, in its January 31, 2005 issue, incredulously observed, "There is almost no precedent for a band's putting out six decent albums and then on its seventh delivering a masterpiece." U.K. rock bible *Q* magazine declared, "The kind of big rock statement rarely heard since the heyday of The Who. This, truly, is the surprise package of 2004." "If Joe Strummer's spirit stalks *American Idiot*, so too does Pete Townshend's. . This is a fully-fledged rock opera—which is almost as chilling a concept as a second Bush term, although Green

Day's muscular grasp of pop verities steers them safely away from conceptual meltdown," *The Guardian* said on September 17, 2004. Major publications as far flung as the *Jerusalem Post* called the album "as ambitious and thought-provoking as anything the band has ever done." *Rolling Stone's* September 20, 2004 review noted, *"Idiot* does a fine job of revving up the basic Green Day conceit, adding emotional flavor to top-shelf Armstrong songs. . .Against all odds, Green Day have found a way to hit their thirties without either betraying their original spirit or falling on their faces." "Years from now, when you want to remember how totally f***ed up the world was in 2004, look no further than the fact that even Green Day felt compelled to write protest songs," *Rolling Stone* observed on December 15, 2004. "The real shocker with *American Idiot*, though, is that what could have been a train wreck—over-the-hill punk-pop trio does rock opera about how the Bush presidency has ruined the country—ranks as the best album the SoCal band has made in years, thanks to a renewed fire in the band's belly and a willingness to extend itself musically." "One of the year's great aural bombshells" and "the best of the band's career" declared the *London Mirror.* U.K. long-stay *NME* on November 20, 2004 wrote, "It ties half a nation's frustration and anger with the 'president gasman' into rock's most ridiculous format and comes out on top." *Billboard* said that the album "is exactly what the band needs to boost itself to the next level," on September 25, 2004. *Kerrang* in July 2004 described it as "An album of punk-rock universality: Thrillingly inventive, defiantly articulate and brilliantly executed." "This is one of the best rock albums and the biggest surprise of the year—a punk rock opera and one of the only mainstream offerings to really address the emotional, moral, and political confusion of our times," observed *Newsweek* in its September 20, 2004 review. To sum up, *Kerrang*, in its 2004 Yearbook issue, declared the album "their masterpiece and, conceivably, *a* masterpiece as well."

Comparisons to Pete Townshend's *Tommy* and the influences of all the greats—from Springsteen to the Sex Pistols, from Bowie to The Beatles—were thrown around in the press. Green Day, however, pointed out some less likely inspiration in the form of the *Rocky Horror Picture Show, West Side Story, Jesus Christ Superstar,* and even *Grease.* The irony of a band that brought three-minute, three-chord songs back to the forefront of the music scene presenting a concept album featuring two nine-minute epics wasn't lost on anyone. After all, weren't punk rock's origins a direct reaction against this sort of thing? The oxymoronic nature of a punk-rock opera was so crazy it couldn't help but fail. But it didn't. It ruled.

The album is a punk rock Zeitgeist, encapsulating the confusion of a disenfranchised generation of young Americans. Centered around a blue-color, lower-middle-class hero called Jesus of Suburbia, the epic storyline weaves its way through his internal struggle, encountering along the way characters St. Jimmy and Whatsername. Confused? To clear it all up, Billie Joe told *Guitar World* in its Holiday 2004 issue, "The constant theme of the record is 'rage versus love.' You can go with the blind rebellion of self-destruction, where St. Jimmy is. But there's a more love-driven side to that, which is following your beliefs and your ethics. And that's where Jesus of Suburbia really wants to go."

The five part "Jesus of Suburbia" was a glorious amalgam of every great rock band that has ever existed while still, ingeniously, remaining pure Green Day. It is a blueprint of sorts for the whole of

American Idiot. How they managed it is beyond most critics, but all were in agreement: This was one of those rare albums that we all subconsciously wait for—earphones at the ready—and never expect. Song after song, it delivered. It was a punk rock state of the nation address.

"Jesus" was a triumph. "It's ridiculous how fun it is to be able to do a nine-minute song with all these changes and different time signatures. It's almost like putting on different clothes for a day," Tré told *Rolling Stone* in its May 26, 2004 edition. Disc jockeys, firstly at L.A.'s KROQ and quickly all over the country introduced the nine-minute track to appreciative listeners. "I think the DJs like 'Jesus of Suburbia' because they can put it on and go have a cigarette and a crap," Tré sacrilegiously commented to MTV on October 1, 2004. OK, let's get serious. As to the album's story line whose main character

is Jesus of Suburbia, Billie Joe told MTV on June 25, 2004, "It's [about] him coming of age and the growing pains that are involved in it and seeing if he makes the right choices or the wrong choices or whatever choices that come to him. . .I developed the character from personal experiences [over the years], but it's definitely set to the political and cultural climate that's going on right now. I am antiwar, so a lot of it has to do with that, and there's also different sides of it too." He told *Stuff* magazine in its October 2004 issue that "a lot of personal experience went into that guy. He feels disenfranchised with his hometown, his school, his family, his friends. He wants to leave town and escape."

The album explores the confusion in an America split right down the middle politically, and the need to find one's individuality once again in the midst of too much information. Disturbed by the play-by-play reporting of the war by imbedded journalists intercut by Viagra commercials, Billie Joe found himself at a songwriting epiphany. Let's not forget, nowadays, parental responsibility tops Billie Joe's list of concerns. The names Joseph and Jakob are tattooed on his forearms. Who would have thought that bratty, foul-mouthed maniac on stage would be monitoring his sons' TV viewing and banning violent video games chez Armstrong? In fact, for someone who burst on the scene by complaining that there was nothing worth watching on TV, Billie Joe finds himself vehemently objecting to a lot of it, such as reality shows chronicling the vapid lives of talentless pop stars or "entertainment" in the form of people eating goat's brains. Worse, however, is that a lot of what's on TV today is downright frightening. The world as we watch it on the box is a far scarier place than it was back in the *Dookie* days.

"What's really at the heart of it is a personal observation of what's going on," Rob Cavallo told the *New York Post* on February 13, 2005. "There hasn't been a record like that in so long—both challenging

intellectually and speaking to kids in a way that helps them define what they're going through as it relates to the cultural and political atmosphere."

Quite an advance from a band that summed up the Bush/Gore political debates back in 2000 as "two guys, one suit." But not so fast. There were seeds of Billie Joe's heightened political awareness cropping up around the time of the release of *Warning*, the band's first album exhibiting political elements. After all, let's not forget that album's promo: A mock presidential campaign. As Billie Joe himself described *Warning* to MTV on October 6, 2000, "It's sort of got commentary [on it] at the same time. There are political overtones to ['Warning']. I mean, nothing really preachy, just sort of what I think about certain issues. But that's all pretty much personal." "If you want to know the truth, do I want to change the world through music?" Billie Joe asked during a December 10, 2000 *Launch* interview. "Well, f*** yeah I want to change the world to a certain extent, yeah. It needs to be changed, it needs a kick in the ass." He brought up politics once again in a *Rolling Stone* interview on October 4, 2004, reflecting, "When you start getting into your politics it's like you have to be vulnerable and you have to be sort of sensitive. Because if it's always like straight aggression all the time, there becomes no empathy for the stance that you're taking. You're not telling people to think, you're telling them what to think."

"It's our most ambitious album to date," Billie Joe told *Rolling Stone* on May 26, 2004. "I wanted to try to find some human relationship throughout it. A lot of it is coming from trying to have a relationship between different people and yourself, but being surrounded by total chaos . . . I didn't want to make people feel like I'm telling them what to do or come across as a sh*tty politician."

Indeed, *American Idiot* does not have to be read in the context of the Bush administration or even of America itself to make sense. It is at once a very current and a very universal piece. Billie Joe has managed to interweave the public with the private. He addresses the death of his father for the first time in song in "Wake Me Up When September Ends," the most intensely personal track on the album. For many, the song will serve as a reflection on 9/11. "For me, September is the month my father died. People's lives tend to go in cycles: The best times and the worst times. And September always ends up being that worst time for me. For some reason, problems always keep cropping up for me in September. It's a heavy month—people are going back to school, there's a change in the weather. . .it feels like the end and the beginning of something much more than December 31," he told *Guitar World* in its February/March 2005 issue. "It's the first time I've written about my father dying when I was ten years old," Billie Joe divulged during a September 7, 2004 MTV interview. "But so there is continuity, I wrote it so it seems like the character is sort of crushed about something, a part where you're looking on your past and you're coming of age at the same time." Much as the band itself had done.

HEART-SHAPED HAND GRENADE

After the intimate precursor, Green Day launched a juggernaut no-holds-barred tour in support of *American Idiot* that would blast its way around the world. The band stepped up the production value of their stage show, involving elaborate lighting, a "fascism"-inspired set design, vast quantities of logo ticker tape, lavish use of pyrotechnics, and outrageous sound. Some elements of big time production, however, don't quite fit in with the Green Day ethic. Sophisticated staging involves complex systems that in the most part must be pre-set. The band's love for throwing the set list out the window presented a bit of a problem, but they were adamant about giving fans the very best show possible without sacrificing their signature spontaneity. "This is really the first time that Green Day has ever used production on this scale," set and lighting designer Justin Collie (of Artfag, a performance environment design company that had worked with many top acts, from Bon Jovi to Korn, and who were at the time double-booked with Green Day and the Beastie Boys) told *Lighting Dimensions* on January 1, 2005. "We ultimately had to come to a compromise with the band because they wanted to be able to play any song at any time. With this much production, you can't do that. Now, we have mapped out certain areas of the set where they can do anything without causing huge problems." The band continued its rebellion against using video during their show—something that most big acts consider an essential. Not Green Day. Their show was big enough without adding what they considered a distraction. The occasional image on a soft-LED drape and an enormous LED sign reading, simply, GREEN DAY, was enough for these punks, thank you.

Billie Joe is a consummate showman. He commands the stage with the full-fledged bravado of rock's greatest. Every inch of his 5'5" frame is put to use as he transforms himself into a punk rock

Tasmanian devil in perpetual motion. He unabashedly borrows from all of rock 'n' rolls greats, wind milling Pete Townshend-style, catapulting himself across the stage with his own version of Chuck Berry's duck walk, and playing his guitar with his teeth just like none other than Jimi Hendrix. Perhaps one day a future rock star will take on a few of Billie Joe's signature performance—facial ticks visible from the back of a stadium, or that arm-breaking assault on his guitar.

The band spent the remainder of 2004 playing victorious sold-out shows across North America with New Found Glory as main support with Southern Californian outfit Sugarcult as the opening act. They played the two-day New Orleans' Voodoo Fest on October 16 and 17 along with sixty acts including the Beastie Boys, Kid Rock, the Killers, the Pixies, and Stone Temple Pilots/Guns 'N Roses hybrid Velvet Revolver. The band were highlights at two December award shows, the *Billboard* Music Awards and the VH-1 Big in '04 Awards show featured performances by Green Day, the Black Eyed Peas, Maroon 5, and Velvet Revolver.

In the days leading up to the U.S. presidential election, Billie Joe performed "American Idiot" in a Bush facemask. During "Holiday" the stage backdrop showed film of bomb-dropping helicopters; Billie Joe introduced the protest song by prefacing that it is not anti-American but rather anti-war. "We see our president and he's like a little kid with his hat and his cowboy boots that are too big for him, and he just doesn't get it. He wants everything his way and he's just a little f***ing brat," Mike told *Kerrang* in its Yearbook 2004 issue. When George W. Bush was re-elected, Tré glibly predicted, "I reckon eventually all these old f***ers who vote for Bush are going to die off and then the younger, cooler generation will vote accordingly," in a March 2005 interview with *Rock Sound*. Billie Joe told *NME* in its November 20, 2004 issue, "I think George Bush is more of a threat to America than Saddam Hussein ever was."

The second single from *American Idiot* was the lush "Boulevard of Broken Dreams." It proved even more popular than its predecessor, reaching the Number One spot on four *Billboard* charts: Adult Top 40, Mainstream Rock Tracks, Modern Rock Tracks, and Top 40 Mainstream; it also hit Number Six on the Top 40 Tracks chart and a very impressive Number Two on the ultimate singles chart, the Hot 100. "Boulevard" also proved to be a mainstay at the top of the list of downloads on iTunes. Green Day pledged to donate all of the band's royalties of the single's iTunes sales to tsunami relief via the Red Cross International Response Fund.

What next? Hollywood anyone? The end of the year also saw rumors of a movie version of Green Day's punk-rock opera. "It's kind of gone from something we had fun talking about to actually getting really serious," Billie Joe told *Billboard* on December 18, 2004. "I'm going to start meeting with some writers and really talk to them about the album. There is room for a lot of dialogue and things like that and taking quotes from the album here and there to put into the script, so it looks like it's going to be a reality."

The latter half of 2004 saw Billie Joe grace the covers of *Total Guitar* and *Guitar World*, Mike was the cover boy for *Total Guitar's* Bass Special and had designed his own signature model Fender bass, and Tré found himself on year-end covers of both U.K. magazine *Drummer* and the U.S.'s *Drum!*

Green Day were being taken very seriously by the music world at large. The end of a landmark year was topped off by not one, not two, but a record six Grammy nominations. *American Idiot* had earned itself the coveted nominations for Album of the Year and Rock Album of the Year. The single of the same name was up for Record of the Year, Best Rock Performance by a Duo or Group with Vocal, Best Rock Song, and Best Short Form Music Video. "The day we heard about the nominations we were playing the Hard Rock in Las Vegas," Billie Joe told *People* in its January 17, 2005 issue. "I put this pair of green-and-purple star-covered underwear over my pants. When I walked in everyone was like, 'Why are you wearing that?' I was like, 'I got six Grammy nominations. I can wear whatever the hell I want.'" The band was stunned but pleased by the industry acknowledgement. "We didn't start playing music to win trophies or anything," Tré told *Entertainment Weekly* in its February 11, 2005 edition. "But it feels really f***in' good to be appreciated." Green Day was up against some tough competition. Ray Charles, who had sadly passed away in June of 2004, was an obvious favorite for Album of the Year, but also in the running was industry darling Alicia Keys, chart-topping R&B big man Usher, and hot new artist Kanye West. "I never thought I'd say this," Billie Joe said to *Time* magazine in its January 31, 2005 issue, "but I'd really like to win Album of the Year. It would be meaningful to me, and without tooting my own horn I kind of think we might even deserve it."

Green Day ushered in 2005 at MTV's Iced Out New Year's Eve star-studded celebration, joining the party with the likes of teeny-popsters of the moment Lindsay Lohan and Ashlee Simpson, Ja Rule, Snoop Dogg, and many others. The band had yet another reason to celebrate as 2005 began, when *American Idiot*—three months after its Number One debut—once again claimed the top spot on the charts knocking heavyweight Eminem's *Encore* down to the Number Two rung on the ladder. The punk opus had now racked up nearly two million sales in the U.S. and over five million worldwide, and its third single, "Holiday" was on its way.

The European leg of the *American Idiot* tour was an outrageous success. The January 12, 2005 gig at the Heineken Music Hall in Amsterdam saw Billie Joe, resplendent in his King of All That Is Punk Rock crown and brandishing an enormous water pistol, addresses the crowd with the zeal of any politician worth their salt, declaring, "No matter what bastard is in power, just think for yourself and never lose your individuality!" Right on, brother.

It was on to the ever-friendly Germany, with a few stops in Spain and France before returning to the U.K. All of the U.K. dates (multiple gigs in England, Ireland, Scotland, and Wales) sold out in one day—which was unprecedented.

Green Day continued their now-legendary tradition of picking audience members out of the crowd for a rousing version of "Knowledge," and Billie Joe found himself giving away Stratocasters like they were Thanksgiving turkeys. Fans were arriving well prepared with signs saying, "Pick Me—I Can Play Guitar!" Of course, it's all very well to wish it was you up there, but one lucky young man made it onstage at London's January 25th Brixton Academy show only to look out at the thousands of faces and promptly throw up. Yep, right on stage. Taking stage fright to an entirely higher level and pretty much determining that rock stardom may not be for him.

On February 5th Green Day played at the seaside town of Brighton, site of the war between the mods and rockers in *Quadrophenia*. The Brighton Centre stand-in guitarist, after being told he could keep

the guitar he had just played in front of a sea of people, stepped up to the mike and said, "I just want to say I love you Billie, I love you Mike, and I love you Tré. And I just want to say thank you, and that I love everyone here tonight." Billie Joe recovered the mike and brought everyone back to punk rock reality with an affectionate "You little f***ing bastard. Coming up here trying to upstage me!"

Green Day commemorated their fourth sold-out London show by playing *American Idiot* straight through. "We always save the best for last," Billie Joe told the Hammersmith Apollo crowd, "So tonight we're going to do something a bit special." Much to the delight of the crowd—*NME's* February 8, 2005 review of the show declared, "The audience reaction remained ecstatic throughout, with a word perfect audience attempting, and sometimes succeeding to outsing the band." It was one of those evenings when Green Day was in an operatic mood. "This whole record was written from a live perspective. If you're not singing in the crowd, then you should be playing air guitar or air drums or something. It's just got that feeling all throughout the record, that type of energy," Mike told MTV on October 18, 2004. As for showcasing it in its entirety, he told *Billboard* on December 7, 2004, "This is something we want to revisit the rest of our career. It's like a new bullet in our arsenal, and it's great to step outside of our regular tour set."

The European tour boosted album sales, and *American Idiot* took the Number One seat on the European Top 100 Albums chart for the first time at the end of January. The album also commanded impressive top ten positions on the country's individual charts: Number Three in Austria, Number

Seven in Germany, Number Four in Greece, Number Seven in Italy, Number One in Sweden and Norway, Number Four in Switzerland, and Number Three in the U.K.

The 47ᵗʰ annual Grammy Awards show was held in Los Angeles at the Staples Center on February 13, 2005. The show was hosted by Queen Latifah and featured performances by Alicia Keys, Tim McGraw, U2, and J-Lo and her latest husband, but it was Green Day's hyperkinetic stint on stage that stole the show. However, it was the late Ray Charles who dominated awards-wise with his final recording, *Genius Loves Company*. Had Ray been alive and well and seated in the front row, it is extremely likely that Green Day may well have gone home with more than one Grammy, one of which being Album of the Year. Nonetheless, it was the first time a punk band had been nominated in the prestigious category. *American Idiot* lost out to "The Genius" Ray in the Record of the Year category as well, and U2's "Vertigo" took the Best Rock Performance by a Duo or Group with Vocal, the Best Short form Music Video, and the Best Rock Song awards. The first ever punk rock opera triumphed, however, by being awarded Best Rock Album, truly a meaningful validation. Yes, Green Day beat out one tough lineup—hot new band the Killers, radio darlings Hoobastank, the Scott Weiland and Slash marriage known as Velvet Revolver, and rock icon Elvis Costello—and took the stage to accept the well-deserved landmark award. Billie Joe, sporting a pinstriped suit and requisite eyeliner, addressed the star-studded crowd and millions watching on their TVs at home, victoriously declaring, "Rock and roll can be dangerous and fun at the same time."

Presumably leaving that groundbreaking Grammy on an Oakland mantelpiece—unless they packed it up with the rest of their gear—the band continued the *American Idiot* world tour, traveling throughout Australia and Japan before returning to the U.S. A month-long North American leg is scheduled commencing April 15ᵗʰ in Miami with My Chemical Romance as support. Green Day has also promised to return to Europe for the summer festival season in June and July 2005. One highlight is sure to be their co-headlining spot alongside the Foo Fighters at Scotland's T in the Park festival. Promoter Geoff Ellis told the *London Mirror* in its February 12, 2005 issue, "It is fantastic to welcome back Green Day to the event—this time in a headline slot. They are one of the hottest and most compelling live acts around today." Most impressive of all is Green Day's double-header at the Milton Keynes National Bowl, which will see Green Day playing to the largest British crowd they have ever entertained in one spot as the venue holds 60,000. One night was originally the plan, but when the huge event sold out, a second date was added.

The Independent Film Channel announced in March 2005 its partnership with Green Day, which will involve the cable TV channel incorporating "Jesus of Suburbia" into its promotions and programming throughout the year. "I.F.C.'s mission is to serve as a safe-haven for free, independent thought," general manager Evan Shapiro told *Business Wire* on March 7, 2005. "We wanted to work with Green Day, because they are the musical personification of that mission—in the era of radio media monopolies, who else writes a nine-minute, five-stanza song cycle?" The unprecedented collaboration affords the song an alternate platform and gives us an indication that Green Day isn't finished stretching conventional pop-music boundaries.

GODFATHERS

It was official. Green Day were the new godfathers of punk rock, the neo-punk elder statesman. On the occasion of the ten-year anniversary of *Dookie's* release, MTV interviewed a few of the new punk outfits that might well owe their very existence to Green Day. *"[Dookie]* changed my life," Joel Madden of Good Charlotte declared. "It made me want to start Good Charlotte. Right after that record came out, we were like, 'We have to start a band in our garage right now and play shows like Green Day." Joel's bandmate Billy Martin remembers his first Green Day experience the way a previous generation remember their earliest exposure to The Beatles, saying, "I came home from school one day, turned on MTV, and the 'Longview' video was the first video I saw. I still had my backpack on and I was standing up. I couldn't sit down because I wanted to wait until the video was over. It was captivating." I was about fourteen when *Dookie* came out," echoed Sum 41's Deryck Whibley. "I remember seeing the video for 'Basket Case' for the first time. I had never heard of Green Day, and then this video came on TV one day. I was so blown away by it. It was so cool. It had so much energy and it was so different. I'd never seen anything like it before. From then I was an instant fan." Steve Klein of New Found Glory concurs. "After I listened to Green Day, it opened a whole new world to me about punk music. I wanted to hear all these different bands just from hearing that record." According to Something Corporate's Josh Partington, *"Dookie* was kind of like the next coming of rock and roll after Nirvana. After *Nevermind,* that was probably the next quintessential album that came out that you had to own to really know what was happening in music."

"With *American Idiot*, Green Day is back to rightfully reclaim the punk/pop throne. In the four years since the band's last studio album, *Warning*, Green Day has watched groups it has clearly influenced, such as Blink-182 and Good Charlotte, try on the punk crown," *Billboard* declared on October 9, 2004. *Rolling Stone's* September 20, 2004 *American Idiot* review observed, "Against all odds, Green Day have found a way to hit their thirties without either betraying their original spirit or falling on their faces. Good Charlotte, you better be taking notes." *Kerrang* observed in its 2004 Yearbook issue that *American Idiot* "raises the bar as to what might reasonably be expected from a modern, mainstream punk-rock album. At least that seems fitting, as this is the group that made the genre mainstream in the first place."

They did something no other punk band is able to do," Tom Calderone, MTV's executive vice president told the *Los Angeles Daily News* on December 12, 2004. "They not only put together a sonic presentation that is unique but still edgy. . .in attitude, but matched it with extremely strong,

mature lyrics. And I think the new kids on the block like Good Charlotte and Simple Plan and New Found Glory should study this album and realize that there is a future beyond three-chord-progression punk rock."

"Punk sometimes has this defeatist attitude where you can't expand," Billie Joe said in a February 11, 2005 *Entertainment Weekly* article. "I look at a band like U2 that started out more or less as a punk band but kept expanding and wound up being one of the biggest bands in the world. And I think it's okay to want that."

How do the Green Day three—after all only in their early thirties—react to the elder statesman label? Mike told MTV on January 7, 2005, "We like a lot of those [young punk] bands, and it's flattering to hear you've influenced them. And all of them are going to forge their own path and catalog and career history some-day. But the compliments are kind of hard to take. It's like, 'Congratulations, you're old!'" Billie Joe wasn't so conflicted. As he told *Entertainment Weekly* in its September 17, 2004 issue in his usual forthright style, "Do I consider myself a leader of this genre? F*** yeah, I do."

American Idiot served as an inauguration for Green Day's punk presidency and rocketed the band to the upper echelons of rock stardom. Billie Joe Armstrong, Mike Dirnt, and Tré Cool have blown the creative and artistic standard out of the water for young punks everywhere, and raised the bar for pop music itself—very, very high. How the hell are they going to follow *that*?

U.S. Discography

EPS

1,000 HOURS
1,000 Hours / Dry Ice / Only of You / The One I Want
Lookout! Records, 1989

SLAPPY
Paper Lanterns / Why Do You Want Him? / 409 in Your
Coffee Maker / Knowledge
Lookout! Records, 1990

SWEET CHILDREN
Sweet Children / Best Thing In Town / Strangeland / My
Generation
Skene! Records, 1990

FULL LENGTH

39/SMOOTH
At the Library / Don't Leave Me / I Was There /
Disappearing Boy / Green Day / Going to Pasalacqua / 16
/ Road to Acceptance / Rest / The Judge's Daughter
Lookout! Records, 1990

1,039/SMOOTHED OUT SLAPPY HOURS
At the Library / Don't Leave Me / I Was There /
Disappearing Boy / Green Day / Going to Pasalacqua / 16
/ Road to Acceptance / Rest / The Judge's Daughter /
Paper Lanterns / Why Do You Want Him? / 409 In Your
Coffee Maker / Knowledge / 1,000 Hours / Dry Ice / Only
of You / The One I Want / I Want to Be Alone
Lookout! Records, 1991

KERPLUNK
2,000 Light Years Away / One for the Razorbacks /
Welcome to Paradise / Christie Road / Private Ale /
Dominated Love Slave / One of My Lies / 80 / Android /
No One Knows / Who Wrote Holden Caulfield? / Words I
Might Have Ate *Plus later added tracks: Sweet Children
/ Best Thing In Town / Strangeland / My Generation
Lookout! Records, 1991

FULL LENGTH continued

DOOKIE

Burnout / Having a Blast / Chump / Longview / Welcome
to Paradise / Pulling Teeth / Basket Case / She / Sassafras
Roots / When I Come Around / Coming Clean / Emenius
Sleepus / In the End / F.O.D. / All By Myself (hidden
track)
Reprise Records, 1994

INSOMNIAC

Armatage Shanks / Brat / Stuck With Me / Geek Stink
Breath / No Pride / Bab's Uvula Who? / 86 / Panic Song /
Stuart and the Ave. / Brain Stew / Jaded / Westbound Sign
/ Tight Wad Hill / Walking Contradiction
Reprise Records, 1995

NIMROD

Nice Guys Finish Last / Hitchin' a Ride / The Grouch /
Redundant / Scattered / All the Time / Worry Rock /
Platypus (I Hate You) / Uptight / Last Ride In / Jinx /
Haushinka / Walking Alone / Reject / Take Back / King
for a Day / Good Riddance (Time of Your Life) /
Prosthetic Head
Reprise Records, 1997

WARNING

Warning / Blood, Sex and Booze / Church on Sunday /
Fashion Victim / Castaway / Misery / Deadbeat Holiday /
Hold On / Jackass / Waiting / Minority / Macy's Day
Parade
Reprise Records, 2000

INTERNATIONAL SUPERHITS!

Maria / Poprocks & Coke / Longview / Welcome to
Paradise / Basket Case / When I Come Around / She /
J.A.R. (Jason Andrew Relva) / Geek Stink Breath / Brain
Stew / Jaded / Walking Contradiction / Stuck with Me /
Hitchin' a Ride / Good Riddance (Time of Your Life) /
Redundant / Nice Guys Finish Last / Minority / Warning /
Waiting / Macy's Day Parade
Reprise Records, 2001

SHENANIGANS

Suffocate / Desensitized / You Lied / Outsider / Don't
Wanna Fall in Love / Espionage / I Want to Be on TV /
Scumbag / Tired of Waiting for You / Sick of Me / Rotting
/ Do Da Da / On the Wagon / Ha Ha You're Dead
Reprise Records, 2002

AMERICAN IDIOT

American Idiot / Jesus of Suburbia (I. Jesus of Suburbia,
II. City of the Damned, III. I Don't Care, IV. Dearly
Beloved, V. Tales of Another Broken Home) / Holiday /
Boulevard of Broken Dreams / Are We the Waiting / St.
Jimmy / Give Me Novacaine / She's a Rebel /
Extraordinary Girl / Letterbomb / Wake Me Up When
September Ends / Homecoming (I. The Death of St.
Jimmy, II. East 12th Street, III. Nobody Likes You, IV.
Rock and Roll Girlfriend, V. We're Coming Home Again)
/ Whatsername
Reprise Records, 2004